JUMBLE®
Jitterbug

Put on Your Jumblin' Shoes!

**Jeff Knurek
and
Mike Argirion**

TRIUMPH
BOOKS

This book is available in quantity at special discounts
for your group or organization.

For further information, contact:

Triumph Books
542 South Dearborn Street
Suite 750
Chicago, Illinois 60605
(312) 939-3330
Fax (312) 663-3557
www.triumphbooks.com

Printed in U.S.A.

ISBN: 978-1-60078-584-9

Design by Sue Knopf

CONTENTS

CLASSIC PUZZLES

DAILY PUZZLES

CHALLENGER PUZZLES

ANSWERS

JUMBLE® *Jitterbug*

Classic Puzzles

JUMBLE®

Unscramble these four Jumbles, one letter to each square, to form four ordinary words.

SYSUF

SCUHR

TEMIKS

JEACKT

Maybe it will improve my footwork

WHY THE BOXER JOINED THE SOCCER TEAM.

Now arrange the circled letters to form the surprise answer, as suggested by the above cartoon.

Ans: " ☐☐☐☐☐ FOR "☐☐☐☐☐☐"

2

JUMBLE®

Unscramble these four Jumbles, one letter to each square, to form four ordinary words.

AKDEB

RUPUS

DECLUD

CADDIN

He's been raised well

WHERE IDEALS CAN COME FROM.

Now arrange the circled letters to form the surprise answer, as suggested by the above cartoon.

Print answer here:

3

PUZZLE
3

JUMBLE®

Unscramble these four Jumbles, one letter to each square, to form four ordinary words.

OMPET

DEWUN

SAHDIR

AFACED

He treats us as equals

Doesn't put on any airs

THE STUDENTS ADMIRED THE ARCHAEOLOGIST BECAUSE HE WAS----

Now arrange the circled letters to form the surprise answer, as suggested by the above cartoon.

Answer: ◯◯◯◯ TO ◯◯◯◯◯

4

JUMBLE®

Unscramble these four Jumbles, one letter to each square, to form four ordinary words.

YERAW

POCHE

FITTOU

FARREY

The new planes will help us expand

WHEN THE CHARTER PILOT'S SON TOOK OVER THE BUSINESS, IT BECAME AN——

Now arrange the circled letters to form the surprise answer, as suggested by the above cartoon.

Answer here:

5

JUMBLE®

Unscramble these four Jumbles, one letter to each square, to form four ordinary words.

PYPIN

SELOO

DOBENY

CAFEED

Now arrange the circled letters to form the surprise answer, as suggested by the above cartoon.

Answer: " ⬡⬡⬡⬡⬡⬡ " ⬡⬡⬡⬡

6

JUMBLE®

Unscramble these four Jumbles, one letter to
each square, to form four ordinary words.

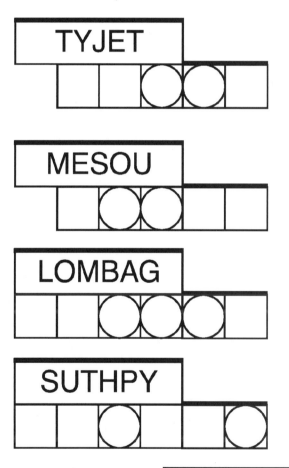

TYJET

MESOU

LOMBAG

SUTHPY

Let's have another round

IN A BAR, SITTING
DOWN CAN RESULT
IN ---

Now arrange the circled letters to form the
surprise answer, as suggested by the above
cartoon.

Answer here:

JUMBLE®

Unscramble these four Jumbles, one letter to
each square, to form four ordinary words.

ELLIB

KIRPE

NUCLUR

ELDAHN

You're fired, you lazy...

ONE RESULT OF
BEING RILED.

Now arrange the circled letters to form the
surprise answer, as suggested by the above
cartoon.

Print answer here:

JUMBLE®

Unscramble these four Jumbles, one letter to each square, to form four ordinary words.

JAHAR

EBBIR

CAFFEE

GOINID

Time for dinner

No time.
Too much work

A BUSY
BLACKSMITH
WILL DO THIS.

Now arrange the circled letters to form the surprise answer, as suggested by the above cartoon.

Ans: " ◯◯◯◯◯ " ◯◯◯◯◯◯

JUMBLE®

Unscramble these four Jumbles, one letter to
each square, to form four ordinary words.

TIFEN

TIMAY

DRAWZI

MILSES

My chest
is moving south

A MIDDLE-AGE
PAUNCH CAN BE A----

Now arrange the circled letters to form the
surprise answer, as suggested by the above
cartoon.

Ans: " ⬤⬤⬤⬤⬤⬤ " OF ⬤⬤⬤⬤

JUMBLE®

Unscramble these four Jumbles, one letter to each square, to form four ordinary words.

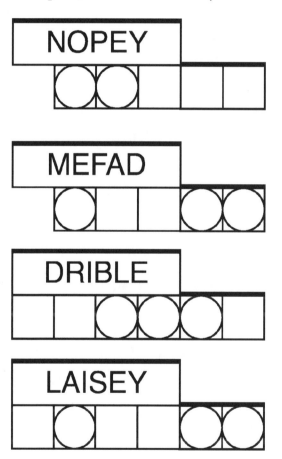

NOPEY

MEFAD

DRIBLE

LAISEY

I'm busy with practice and homework

WHY THE YOUNG BALL PLAYER DIDN'T HAVE A STEADY GIRLFRIEND.

Now arrange the circled letters to form the surprise answer, as suggested by the above cartoon.

A: HE ⃝⃝⃝⃝⃝⃝ THE " ⃝⃝⃝⃝⃝ "

11

JUMBLE®

Unscramble these four Jumbles, one letter to each square, to form four ordinary words.

CEDDI
◯◯ □ □ ◯

GIHLT
◯◯ □ ◯ □

LAIFAC
◯ □ ◯ ◯ □ □

TIGBLE
◯ □ □ □ ◯ ◯

Happy Birthday!

Oh, boy. It's a kind of computer

GIVING JUNIOR A HEAP OF EDUCA-TIONAL TOYS MADE HIM A---

Now arrange the circled letters to form the surprise answer, as suggested by the above cartoon.

A: " ◯◯◯◯◯◯ " ◯◯◯◯◯

JUMBLE®

Unscramble these four Jumbles, one letter to
each square, to form four ordinary words.

BASAH

MARAD

STINCH

BROSAB

THE SECRETARY
CONCENTRATED
ON THIS.

Now arrange the circled letters to form the
surprise answer, as suggested by the above
cartoon.

Answer: THE ⬡⬡⬡⬡⬡⬡ ⬡⬡⬡⬡

JUMBLE®

Unscramble these four Jumbles, one letter to each square, to form four ordinary words.

VALIT

YOVIR

BINLEB

ANGOLS

My neck hurts from looking up

WATCHING AN IRONWORKER HIGH ON A SKYSCRAPER CAN BE----

Now arrange the circled letters to form the surprise answer, as suggested by the above cartoon.

Answer here: "  "

14

JUMBLE®

Unscramble these four Jumbles, one letter to each square, to form four ordinary words.

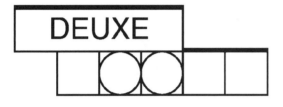
DEUXE

TILMI

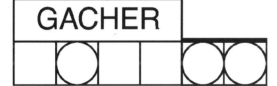
GACHER

YAUNES

Whew, that was a tough one

WHEN THE MECHANIC INSTALLED THE NEW MUFFLER, IT WAS---

Now arrange the circled letters to form the surprise answer, as suggested by the above cartoon.

Ans: " ◯◯◯◯◯◯◯◯◯◯◯ "

JUMBLE®

Unscramble these four Jumbles, one letter to each square, to form four ordinary words.

OGOIL

NEKEL

WURPAD

KLYFNU

Oh my! It's gorgeous

I love it

WHEN SHE CHANGED HER HAIR COLOR, IT WAS----

Now arrange the circled letters to form the surprise answer, as suggested by the above cartoon.

Print answer here: TO "  "

JUMBLE®

Unscramble these four Jumbles, one letter to
each square, to form four ordinary words.

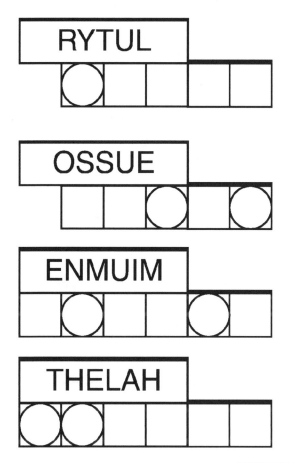

RYTUL

OSSUE

ENMUIM

THELAH

Your eggs, gentlemen

Let's look over
this report

WHAT THE
BUSINESSMEN
READ BEFORE
BREAKFAST.

Now arrange the circled letters to form the
surprise answer, as suggested by the above
cartoon.

Print answer here:

17

PUZZLE
17

JUMBLE®

Unscramble these four Jumbles, one letter to
each square, to form four ordinary words.

TCHAB

NOPER

RUBECH

SMALEY

Let's lie in the sun
until our hair dries

WHAT THE TEEN-
AGERS TURNED
INTO AFTER A DIP
IN THE OCEAN.

Now arrange the circled letters to form the
surprise answer, as suggested by the above
cartoon.

A:

18

JUMBLE®

Unscramble these four Jumbles, one letter to each square, to form four ordinary words.

ENDUC

ZENOO

REZIFE

HUBILS

The one and only...

WHEN THE CATS
PERFORMED
FOR THE ANIMAL
TRAINER, HE WAS----

Now arrange the circled letters to form the surprise answer, as suggested by the above cartoon.

Answer here: " ◯◯◯◯◯◯◯◯◯ "

JUMBLE®

Unscramble these four Jumbles, one letter to each square, to form four ordinary words.

ORVAS

HIWSS

LENGAC

LAMAMM

It is the very fiber of my work

WHEN THE ARTIST WAS ASKED WHAT WAS BEHIND THE PAINTING, HE SAID IT---

Now arrange the circled letters to form the surprise answer, as suggested by the above cartoon.

Answer: ☐☐☐ A ☐☐☐☐☐☐

JUMBLE®

Unscramble these four Jumbles, one letter to each square, to form four ordinary words.

CNOTH

TAULD

TOGIER

SOYRAV

Watch me.
Then keep
practicing

WHEN THE BALLET
STAR HELPED HER
DANCEMATE, SHE
DID A----

Now arrange the circled letters to form the surprise answer, as suggested by the above cartoon.

Answer here: ⬡⬡⬡⬡ " ⬡⬡⬡⬡ "

JUMBLE ®

Unscramble these four Jumbles, one letter to
each square, to form four ordinary words.

VARGE

BOSEE

BABRYC

SMIBUT

Looks like
kids did it

WHEN VANDALS
USED SPRAY PAINT
ON THE STEPS,
POLICE SAID IT
WAS---

Now arrange the circled letters to form the
surprise answer, as suggested by the above
cartoon.

Ans: A ◯◯◯◯◯◯ " ◯◯◯◯ "

JUMBLE®

Unscramble these four Jumbles, one letter to each square, to form four ordinary words.

LIWLT

CHARP

DEECES

TEAZOL

Not my style

WHY THE YOUNG KING REFUSED TO WEAR A CROWN.

Now arrange the circled letters to form the surprise answer, as suggested by the above cartoon.

Ans: IT ☐☐☐ ☐☐☐ " ☐☐☐ "

JUMBLE®

Unscramble these four Jumbles, one letter to each square, to form four ordinary words.

BADIE

DONSY

BADCUT

GRUNNE

This isn't my favorite chore

WHEN MOM SEWED THE HOLE IN HIS SOCK, SHE CON- SIDERED IT A---

Now arrange the circled letters to form the surprise answer, as suggested by the above cartoon.

A: " ⬡⬡⬡⬡ " ⬡⬡⬡⬡⬡⬡⬡⬡

PUZZLE
24

JUMBLE®

Unscramble these four Jumbles, one letter to each square, to form four ordinary words.

KAYWG

KULCC

HARTTO

NURTAT

Where did he come from?

WHEN THE PHONY TRAPEZE ARTIST FELL INTO THE NET, HE WAS---

Now arrange the circled letters to form the surprise answer, as suggested by the above cartoon.

Ans: [⃝⃝⃝⃝⃝⃝⃝] IN THE " [⃝⃝⃝] "

25

PUZZLE
25

JUMBLE®

Unscramble these four Jumbles, one letter to each square, to form four ordinary words.

GLUHC

CAPIN

RECUPS

SCIBEP

Home of the one-minute haircut

WHEN THE CREW
LINED UP FOR
HAIRCUTS, THE
SUBMARINE
BECAME---

Now arrange the circled letters to form the surprise answer, as suggested by the above cartoon.

A: A "⬡⬡⬡⬡⬡⬡⬡" ⬡⬡⬡⬡

26

JUMBLE®
Jitterbug

Daily
Puzzles

JUMBLE®

Unscramble these four Jumbles, one letter to each square, to form four ordinary words.

CUPAN

ROLYG

SILCHE

LOTTEB

C'mon, Stretch. Time to get up

WHAT THE TALLEST PLAYER DID WHEN THE TEAM STAYED IN A HOTEL.

Now arrange the circled letters to form the surprise answer, as suggested by the above cartoon.

A: ◯◯◯◯◯ " ◯◯◯◯◯◯ "

28

JUMBLE®

Unscramble these four Jumbles, one letter to each square, to form four ordinary words.

RUHTT

ILPAT

FOUNSI

LISGRY

Sorry, sir. Can't find it

!!@?
Of all the incompetent...

WHAT HAPPENED WHEN HIS GRIP WAS LOST.

Now arrange the circled letters to form the surprise answer, as suggested by the above cartoon.

A: HE ⃝⃝⃝⃝ ⃝⃝⃝ " ⃝⃝⃝⃝ "

29

JUMBLE®

Unscramble these four Jumbles, one letter to each square, to form four ordinary words.

YONIR

WHEGI

HYWINN

NAUSED

Go buy yourself something

That's a $2,000 pot

SHE WAS ATTRACTED TO THE CARD SHARK BECAUSE HE HAD---

Now arrange the circled letters to form the surprise answer, as suggested by the above cartoon.

A: " ⬡⬡⬡⬡⬡⬡ " ⬡⬡⬡⬡

30

JUMBLE®

Unscramble these four Jumbles, one letter to each square, to form four ordinary words.

KREPY

HELAT

DRALIA

SPELTE

IN THE OLD WEST, A SIX-SHOOTER WAS AN ---

Now arrange the circled letters to form the surprise answer, as suggested by the above cartoon.

A: ⭘⭘⭘⭘⭘ " ⭘⭘⭘⭘⭘⭘⭘ "

JUMBLE®

Unscramble these four Jumbles, one letter to each square, to form four ordinary words.

VEALE

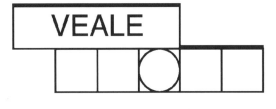

PODEK

FISHTE

RAMTRY

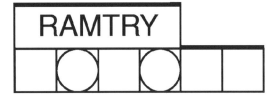

I'll never get married again

Goodbye!

SHE DUMPED HER BOYFRIEND BE-CAUSE SHE WANTED A FUTURE AND HE----

Now arrange the circled letters to form the surprise answer, as suggested by the above cartoon.

Print answer here: ◯◯◯ A ◯◯◯◯◯

JUMBLE®

Unscramble these four Jumbles, one letter to
each square, to form four ordinary words.

ROPIR

SIFIN

FITANN

MELING

They used to
cost a quarter

$2.00

WHY THE
BALLOONS
WENT UP.

Now arrange the circled letters to form the
surprise answer, as suggested by the above
cartoon.

Answer: " ⭕⭕⭕⭕⭕⭕⭕⭕⭕⭕ "

33

JUMBLE®

Unscramble these four Jumbles, one letter to
each square, to form four ordinary words.

ILLSE

DIMAT

CHETOL

THINGK

Another round
on me

Jim always buys

BEING LOOSE WITH
MONEY CAN LEAD
TO THIS.

Now arrange the circled letters to form the
surprise answer, as suggested by the above
cartoon.

Ans: " ◯◯◯◯◯ " ◯◯◯◯◯◯

34

JUMBLE®

Unscramble these four Jumbles, one letter to each square, to form four ordinary words.

UNEES

KALFE

JOADIN

FRIVEY

THE REFEREE
THOUGHT THE
DEFENSIVE LINEMAN
WAS---

Now arrange the circled letters to form the surprise answer, as suggested by the above cartoon.

Answer here:

34

JUMBLE®

Unscramble these four Jumbles, one letter to each square, to form four ordinary words.

MOROG

DYRYL

POONUC

VINTEN

I'm starting to sweat

Just a couple more shots

EASY TO BECOME WHEN MODELING FUR COATS.

Now arrange the circled letters to form the surprise answer, as suggested by the above cartoon.

Ans: A " ◯◯◯◯◯ " ◯◯◯◯

36

JUMBLE®

Unscramble these four Jumbles, one letter to each square, to form four ordinary words.

NUDOM

SBELS

SOLFIS

HEWZEE

I can't afford a minute's rest

GO NUTS FOR DOUGHNUTS

WHEN THE DOUGH-NUT MAKER BOUGHT OUT HIS PARTNER, HE GOT THE ----

Now arrange the circled letters to form the surprise answer, as suggested by the above cartoon.

A: " ⬯⬯⬯⬯ " ⬯⬯⬯⬯⬯⬯⬯⬯

JUMBLE®

Unscramble these four Jumbles, one letter to each square, to form four ordinary words.

TILUQ

ELTAM

IGGLOO

GNININ

I saw the light!

HOW THE ELEC-
TRICIAN DESCRIBED
THE PREACHER'S
SERMON.

Now arrange the circled letters to form the surprise answer, as suggested by the above cartoon.

A: "◯◯◯◯◯◯◯◯◯◯◯◯◯◯"

JUMBLE®

Unscramble these four Jumbles, one letter to each square, to form four ordinary words.

COVAL

MYRIG

CHINLE

SLUDOH

He's so fast   and handsome

THE CHEERLEADER
SAID HER BEAU,
THE SPRINTER,
WAS---

Now arrange the circled letters to form the surprise answer, as suggested by the above cartoon.

Answer here: " ◯◯◯◯◯◯◯ "

PUZZLE
38

JUMBLE®

Unscramble these four Jumbles, one letter to
each square, to form four ordinary words.

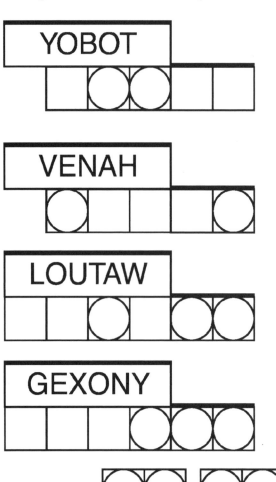

YOBOT

VENAH

LOUTAW

GEXONY

Hi, my name is Ted and...

WHERE HE WENT
WHEN HE STOPPED
DRINKING.

Now arrange the circled letters to form the
surprise answer, as suggested by the above
cartoon.

Answer: ◯◯ ◯◯◯ ◯◯◯◯◯

40

JUMBLE®

Unscramble these four Jumbles, one letter to
each square, to form four ordinary words.

CENIE

EVVAL

DEMIPE

SHIGLE

LEATHER

The dogs will lose
my scent in here

THE ESCAPEE BROKE
INTO THE
TANNERY BECAUSE
IT WAS A---

Now arrange the circled letters to form the
surprise answer, as suggested by the above
cartoon.

A: " ⬡⬡⬡⬡⬡⬡⬡ " ⬡⬡⬡⬡⬡⬡

JUMBLE®

Unscramble these four Jumbles, one letter to
each square, to form four ordinary words.

IXTYS

ONLOY

ROTHEY

KHENAS

Jimmy,
stop that!

Oh, he's
just playing

WHAT THE BOXER DID
WHEN HIS GIRL-
FRIEND'S LITTLE
BROTHER APPEARED.

Now arrange the circled letters to form the
surprise answer, as suggested by the above
cartoon.

A: ⬚⬚⬚⬚⬚ IT
ON ⬚⬚⬚⬚ ⬚⬚⬚⬚⬚

42

JUMBLE®

Unscramble these four Jumbles, one letter to
each square, to form four ordinary words.

CEWTI

LODOF

PALLOW

YANNCO

Utilities are extra,
2 months deposit,
no pets

WHAT THE TENANT
GOT WHEN HE RENTED
THE BASEMENT
APARTMENT.

Now arrange the circled letters to form the
surprise answer, as suggested by the above
cartoon.

Answer: THE "◯◯◯-◯◯◯◯"

43

JUMBLE®

Unscramble these four Jumbles, one letter to each square, to form four ordinary words.

CANKS

SYBSA

YURCOT

EVILAB

The cheerleaders are quite lovely

A GOOD WAY TO IMPROVE THE VIEW AT A FOOTBALL GAME.

Now arrange the circled letters to form the surprise answer, as suggested by the above cartoon.

Answer:

44

JUMBLE®

Unscramble these four Jumbles, one letter to each square, to form four ordinary words.

KLANB

TINJO

BYBURG

ROUGAC

I'm going to buy a bike

.99

FILLING THE GAS TANK THESE DAYS CAN LEAVE YOU ----

Now arrange the circled letters to form the surprise answer, as suggested by the above cartoon.

Answer here: " ◯◯◯◯◯◯◯ "

JUMBLE®

Unscramble these four Jumbles, one letter to each square, to form four ordinary words.

RAUZE

YLSYH

WURFOR

TUFACE

WHEN THE MANAGER KEPT CHANGING PITCHERS, THE SOUTHPAW ---

Now arrange the circled letters to form the surprise answer, as suggested by the above cartoon.

Answer here: ⬡⬡⬡ " ⬡⬡⬡⬡ "

JUMBLE®

Unscramble these four Jumbles, one letter to each square, to form four ordinary words.

TAFAL

ADDEJ

CLINEY

TRAVOC

Maybe we shouldn't get married

Don't tell me how to drive!

WHEN HER FIANCE GOT HOT UNDER THE COLLAR, SHE ENDED UP WITH ---

Now arrange the circled letters to form the surprise answer, as suggested by the above cartoon.

Answer here:

JUMBLE

Unscramble these four Jumbles, one letter to each square, to form four ordinary words.

CAPHO

STATY

DASSIT

SAMIPH

He embezzled bank funds

THE CONVICT
ENJOYED SITTING
IN THE SUN BECAUSE
HE HAD A ---

Now arrange the circled letters to form the surprise answer, as suggested by the above cartoon.

Answer: "◯◯◯◯◯◯" ◯◯◯◯

JUMBLE®

Unscramble these four Jumbles, one letter to each square, to form four ordinary words.

TOROB

TEQUS

ZERTHI

ACNIPT

You belong in this beauty

Can I have your autograph?

WHEN THE EX-STRIKEOUT KING SOLD CARS, HE USED HIS – – –

Now arrange the circled letters to form the surprise answer, as suggested by the above cartoon.

Answer: ⬡⬡⬡⬡ " ⬡⬡⬡⬡⬡ "

JUMBLE®

Unscramble these four Jumbles, one letter to
each square, to form four ordinary words.

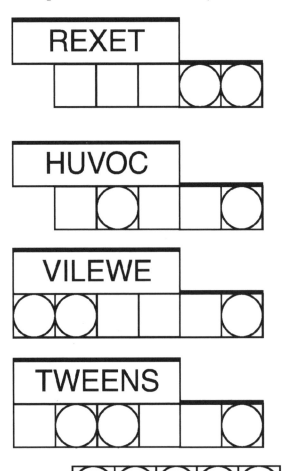

REXET

HUVOC

VILEWE

TWEENS

Not enough business

CLOSING SALE

SALE

10
DAYS
LEFT

WHAT THE BATH
SHOP DID WHEN
BUSINESS SOURED

Now arrange the circled letters to form the
surprise answer, as suggested by the above
cartoon.

Ans:  IN THE

JUMBLE®

Unscramble these four Jumbles, one letter to
each square, to form four ordinary words.

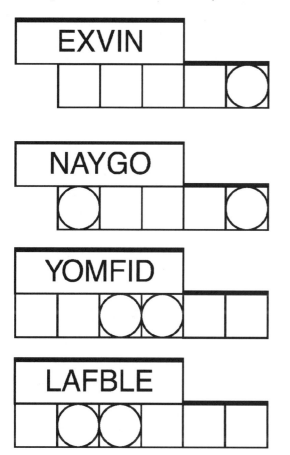

EXVIN

NAYGO

YOMFID

LAFBLE

Guilty!
$50.00.
Next!

FOR A TRAFFIC
COURT JUDGE, IT'S
ALWAYS A ---

Now arrange the circled letters to form the
surprise answer, as suggested by the above
cartoon.

Print answer here: "  "

PUZZLE
50

JUMBLE®

Unscramble these four Jumbles, one letter to
each square, to form four ordinary words.

GEBOF

BODUT

CONARY

ENGOBY

Do I hear
$2,500?

That's enough.
Let's go

WHAT HE BID
AT THE AUCTION

Now arrange the circled letters to form the
surprise answer, as suggested by the above
cartoon.

Print answer here: ⬡⬡⬡⬡ ⬡⬡⬡

JUMBLE®

Unscramble these four Jumbles, one letter to each square, to form four ordinary words.

KANTE

UMPEL

UNMOLC

DINCUT

The saw is stuck again

You're through!

THE CARPENTER FIRED HIS HELPER BECAUSE HE ---

Now arrange the circled letters to form the surprise answer, as suggested by the above cartoon.

A: ⬡⬡⬡⬡⬡⬡⬡ ' ⬡ " ⬡⬡⬡ " IT

PUZZLE
52

JUMBLE®

Unscramble these four Jumbles, one letter to
each square, to form four ordinary words.

GNUST

SHIWK

UNMUTA

PORTIM

I'll see you
in court!

WHEN THE CLEANER
RUINED THE
LAWYER'S OUTFIT,
HE FACED A ‒ ‒ ‒

Now arrange the circled letters to form the
surprise answer, as suggested by the above
cartoon.

Answer here:

54

JUMBLE®

Unscramble these four Jumbles, one letter to
each square, to form four ordinary words.

VOABE

HOTOT

RUPALL

ATTARR

You're three hours late

EASY TO GET
WITHOUT A LOT
OF TROUBLE

Now arrange the circled letters to form the
surprise answer, as suggested by the above
cartoon.

A: A ☐☐☐ OF ☐☐☐☐☐☐☐

JUMBLE®

Unscramble these four Jumbles, one letter to each square, to form four ordinary words.

SCEAT

KAQUE

SCYTIK

NESSUC

What concentration

His hands are magical

WHEN THE CONCERT PIANIST PERFORMED HE EXHIBITED HIS ---

Now arrange the circled letters to form the surprise answer, as suggested by the above cartoon.

A: " ⃝⃝⃝⃝ " TO ⃝⃝⃝⃝⃝⃝⃝⃝

PUZZLE
55

JUMBLE®

Unscramble these four Jumbles, one letter to each square, to form four ordinary words.

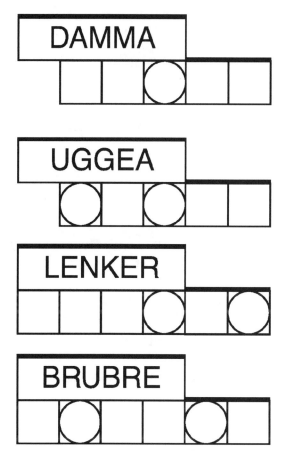

DAMMA

UGGEA

LENKER

BRUBRE

Wow! She's gorgeous

She won't give you the time of day

ALTHOUGH SHE WAS STUCK-UP, HER LOOKS MADE HIM ---

Now arrange the circled letters to form the surprise answer, as suggested by the above cartoon.

Print answer here: "  "

JUMBLE®

Unscramble these four Jumbles, one letter to
each square, to form four ordinary words.

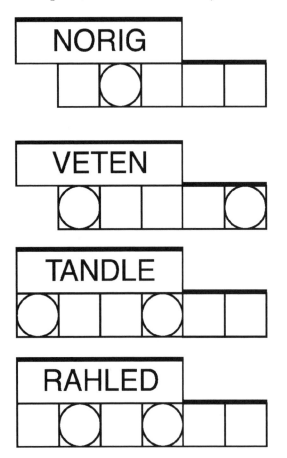

NORIG

VETEN

TANDLE

RAHLED

No big deal.
It's on me

Thanks.
Send me
the bill

WHEN THE DOCTOR
DIDN'T CHARGE
HIM, THE YOUNG
PATIENT WAS ----

Now arrange the circled letters to form the
surprise answer, as suggested by the above
cartoon.

Print answer here: "  "

JUMBLE®

Unscramble these four Jumbles, one letter to each square, to form four ordinary words.

MYDUP

PUMIO

LAWHOL

NOYKED

You're the best player

Can we have your autograph?

WHAT THE SCHOOL-BOYS DID WHEN THEY MET THE BASKETBALL STAR

Now arrange the circled letters to form the surprise answer, as suggested by the above cartoon.

A: ⬡⬡⬡⬡⬡⬡ " ⬡⬡ " TO ⬡⬡⬡

59

JUMBLE®

Unscramble these four Jumbles, one letter to each square, to form four ordinary words.

NELLK

CRAID

LUWANT

LIKALA

He's the runaway favorite

VOTE!

CARL for MAYOR

HOW THE BAKER WON THE TOWN ELECTION

Now arrange the circled letters to form the surprise answer, as suggested by the above cartoon.

Ans: ⬡⬡ A ⬡⬡⬡⬡⬡⬡⬡⬡⬡

60

JUMBLE®

Unscramble these four Jumbles, one letter to each square, to form four ordinary words.

NACEP

THACC

HOIDAR

FEXPIR

Here's our honeymoon suite

WHAT THE GROOM DID WHEN HE MARRIED THE MATH TEACHER

Now arrange the circled letters to form the surprise answer, as suggested by the above cartoon.

A: ◯◯◯◯◯◯◯◯ THE " ◯◯◯ "

JUMBLE®

Unscramble these four Jumbles, one letter to each square, to form four ordinary words.

HIFAT

APROV

DOUSEX

NAHDDE

This is a big job

Call someone

THE OWNER DIDN'T REPAIR THE ROOF BECAUSE IT WAS ----

Now arrange the circled letters to form the surprise answer, as suggested by the above cartoon.

Ans:

JUMBLE ®

Unscramble these four Jumbles, one letter to each square, to form four ordinary words.

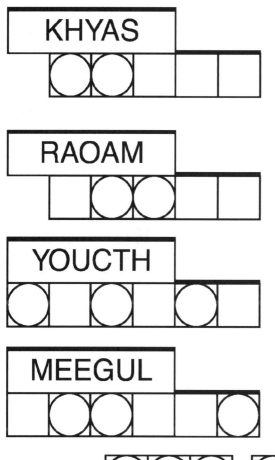

KHYAS

RAOAM

YOUCTH

MEEGUL

THE KIND OF DRESS WORN BY A GHOST

Now arrange the circled letters to form the surprise answer, as suggested by the above cartoon.

Answer: ◯◯◯ - ◯◯◯◯◯◯◯◯

JUMBLE®

Unscramble these four Jumbles, one letter to
each square, to form four ordinary words.

SHEWO

GOBUH

LOCSRL

KADMAS

Ask him.
He reads
everything

Do you know
of a good mystery?

FICTION

INFORMATION

WHAT HE USED WHEN
HE WAS FISHING FOR
A GOOD NOVEL

Now arrange the circled letters to form the
surprise answer, as suggested by the above
cartoon.

Answer here: A

JUMBLE®

Unscramble these four Jumbles, one letter to each square, to form four ordinary words.

DROUG

MALUB

REVEWS

PHEPOR

300!
I can't believe it

WHEN HE ROLLED
A PERFECT GAME,
HE WAS ---

Now arrange the circled letters to form the surprise answer, as suggested by the above cartoon.

Ans: " ◯◯◯◯◯◯◯ " ◯◯◯◯◯

JUMBLE®

Unscramble these four Jumbles, one letter to each square, to form four ordinary words.

RARIF

ADDIE

YAWMID

BOLIFE

Hello you beautiful doll

AAWK

He has quite a vocabulary

HOW HE DESCRIBED HIS PARROT

Now arrange the circled letters to form the surprise answer, as suggested by the above cartoon.

A: A

JUMBLE®

Unscramble these four Jumbles, one letter to each square, to form four ordinary words.

ZAWLT

HYDUC

INDAGE

SIMREY

They're biting by the weeds

This will make good eating

WHERE YOU CAN FIND THE MOST FISH

Now arrange the circled letters to form the surprise answer, as suggested by the above cartoon.

Answer: IN ◯◯◯ ◯◯◯◯◯◯

PUZZLE
66

JUMBLE®

Unscramble these four Jumbles, one letter to each square, to form four ordinary words.

RINPT

VANKE

STRAIG

SATHAG

It took forever to find it

It's perfect

WHAT THE COUPLE WENT THROUGH BUYING THE RIGHT HOUSE

Now arrange the circled letters to form the surprise answer, as suggested by the above cartoon.

A:

68

JUMBLE®

Unscramble these four Jumbles, one letter to each square, to form four ordinary words.

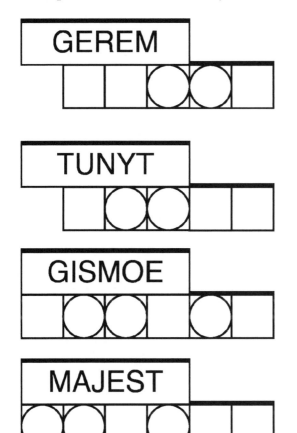

GEREM

TUNYT

GISMOE

MAJEST

What a sight

HOW THE COUPLE DESCRIBED THE GRAND CANYON

Now arrange the circled letters to form the surprise answer, as suggested by the above cartoon.

Ans: ⟨○○○○○⟩ " ⟨○○○○○○○⟩ "

69

JUMBLE®

Unscramble these four Jumbles, one letter to each square, to form four ordinary words.

FARIE

TYDIT

SULUFE

ARPITE

Watch out for stumps

Oops!

WHAT THE SCOUT EXPERIENCED WHEN HE HIKED THROUGH THE WOODS

Now arrange the circled letters to form the surprise answer, as suggested by the above cartoon.

Ans: A 〇〇〇〇〇 " 〇〇〇〇 "

JUMBLE®

Unscramble these four Jumbles, one letter to each square, to form four ordinary words.

POREA

NAJOB

BRATIL

WABUSY

I was safe!   You were out!

WHEN THE PLAYERS BEGAN FIGHTING, THE GAME TURNED INTO ---

Now arrange the circled letters to form the surprise answer, as suggested by the above cartoon.

Answer here:

JUMBLE®

Unscramble these four Jumbles, one letter to each square, to form four ordinary words.

NESOO

SPEHE

TRIEHD

TUVIRE

ON YOUR FEET!
Your boots are filthy

WHAT THE SARGE
SAID TO THE
SLEEPING RECRUIT

Now arrange the circled letters to form the surprise answer, as suggested by the above cartoon.

Answer: ⃝⃝⃝⃝ AND ⃝⃝⃝⃝⃝

JUMBLE®

Unscramble these four Jumbles, one letter to each square, to form four ordinary words.

UPYTT

SLARN

NOCABE

KABETS

Just a temporary market adjustment

My portfolio is down 15%

WHAT THE BROKER GAVE THE NERVOUS INVESTOR

Now arrange the circled letters to form the surprise answer, as suggested by the above cartoon.

A: A " ◯◯◯◯◯ " ◯◯◯◯◯◯

73

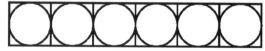

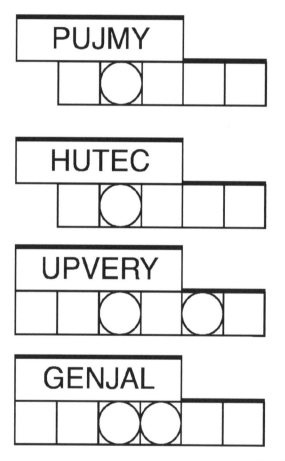

JUMBLE

Unscramble these four Jumbles, one letter to each square, to form four ordinary words.

PUJMY

HUTEC

UPVERY

GENJAL

What a lovely. presentation

I'm starved

NO MATTER WHAT IS SERVED, THIS WILL MAKE IT ATTRACTIVE.

Now arrange the circled letters to form the surprise answer, as suggested by the above cartoon.

Print answer here: ◯◯◯◯◯◯

JUMBLE®

Unscramble these four Jumbles, one letter to each square, to form four ordinary words.

ASTEE

CYRUR

PORTSY

USDABE

Any problems
bring it back

SALE

THE MATTRESS WAS
GUARANTEED SO
THE COUPLE
COULD ---

Now arrange the circled letters to form the surprise answer, as suggested by the above cartoon.

A: " ⬭⬭⬭⬭ " ⬭⬭⬭⬭⬭⬭⬭

JUMBLE®

Unscramble these four Jumbles, one letter to each square, to form four ordinary words.

YENEM

DESET

LESPEN

GOYAVE

Oh, look at those cute shoes

Yes, dear

WINDOW-SHOPPING WITH HIS WIFE LEFT HIM ----

Now arrange the circled letters to form the surprise answer, as suggested by the above cartoon.

Ans: " ⬭⬭⬭⬭⬭⬭ " ⬭⬭⬭⬭

JUMBLE®

Unscramble these four Jumbles, one letter to each square, to form four ordinary words.

PLITO

ROGGE

PRUMBE

SUDSIC

It looks so real. I love it

OOTTAT

WHEN THE TATTOO ARTIST PUT A BUTTERFLY ON HER LEG, SHE WAS ---

Now arrange the circled letters to form the surprise answer, as suggested by the above cartoon.

Answer: " ◯◯◯◯◯◯◯◯◯ "

PUZZLE
76

JUMBLE®

Unscramble these four Jumbles, one letter to each square, to form four ordinary words.

SATHY

TRAFE

RESHOK

PYGINT

You need a short curly look

WHAT THE HAIR-DRESSER DID FOR THE LONG-HAIRED BRUNETTE.

Now arrange the circled letters to form the surprise answer, as suggested by the above cartoon.

Answer: " ⬡⬡⬡ " HER ⬡⬡⬡⬡⬡

78

JUMBLE®

Unscramble these four Jumbles, one letter to
each square, to form four ordinary words.

MUNAH

GEDEW

NETEOD

REYHEB

Dig it.
Plant it.
Do it again.

THE FARMER'S
SIMPLE PHILOSOPHY
WAS ---

Now arrange the circled letters to form the
surprise answer, as suggested by the above
cartoon.

Ans: ⬡⬡⬡⬡ TO " ⬡⬡⬡⬡⬡ "

JUMBLE®

Unscramble these four Jumbles, one letter to each square, to form four ordinary words.

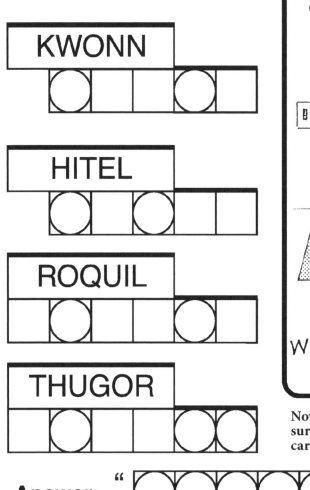

KWONN

HITEL

ROQUIL

THUGOR

Take it easy

WHAT THE ELECTRICIAN DID WHILE HE RECOVERED FROM HIS INJURY.

Now arrange the circled letters to form the surprise answer, as suggested by the above cartoon.

Answer: "  "

JUMBLE®

Unscramble these four Jumbles, one letter to
each square, to form four ordinary words.

TACHY

TIDIO

BABFLY

TEMRIP

I enjoy spending
time with you

He could
be the one

WHEN THEY MET
ON HORSEBACK,
SHE WAS ON THE ----

Now arrange the circled letters to form the
surprise answer, as suggested by the above
cartoon.

Ans: " ⃝⃝⃝⃝⃝⃝ " ⃝⃝⃝⃝

81

JUMBLE®

Unscramble these four Jumbles, one letter to each square, to form four ordinary words.

TUINY

SOSBA

RECLEY

LEMITY

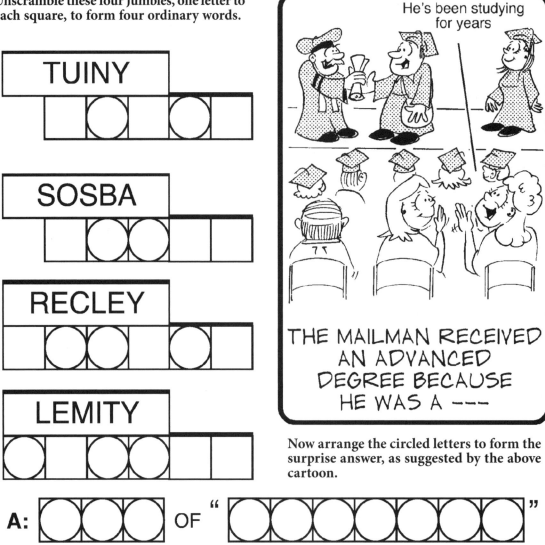

He's been studying for years

THE MAILMAN RECEIVED AN ADVANCED DEGREE BECAUSE HE WAS A ---

Now arrange the circled letters to form the surprise answer, as suggested by the above cartoon.

A: [◯◯◯] OF " [◯◯◯◯◯◯◯] "

JUMBLE®

Unscramble these four Jumbles, one letter to each square, to form four ordinary words.

DRIAP

PYTEM

DIALIN

PLOUCE

STREET FESTIVAL

My foot is killing me

POI

WHAT SHE EXPERIENCED WHEN SHE DANCED IN HER NEW SHOES.

Now arrange the circled letters to form the surprise answer, as suggested by the above cartoon.

Answer: ◯◯◯◯ AT THE "◯◯◯◯"

PUZZLE
82

JUMBLE®

Unscramble these four Jumbles, one letter to
each square, to form four ordinary words.

DUPON

DALIP

HUCNAH

FEWLOU

They're trying
to catch the
bank robbers

What's the delay?

THE POLICE
ROADBLOCK
LED TO A ---

Now arrange the circled letters to form the
surprise answer, as suggested by the above
cartoon.

A:

JUMBLE®

Unscramble these four Jumbles, one letter to each square, to form four ordinary words.

PLUJE

ACOME

RUPPLE

BOTERD

I need parts for my '54 Nash

WHAT THE FARMER SAW WHEN HE VISITED THE JUNKYARD.

Now arrange the circled letters to form the surprise answer, as suggested by the above cartoon.

A: A " ◯◯◯◯◯◯◯ " ◯◯◯◯

85

JUMBLE®

Unscramble these four Jumbles, one letter to each square, to form four ordinary words.

OVEEK

LAUFT

SNUFIL

FROGLE

He's handsome and he's building another subdivision

SHE CHASED THE REAL ESTATE DEVELOPER BECAUSE HE HAD ----

Now arrange the circled letters to form the surprise answer, as suggested by the above cartoon.

Ans: " ◯◯◯◯ " TO ◯◯◯◯◯

JUMBLE®

Unscramble these four Jumbles, one letter to each square, to form four ordinary words.

LEKAN

TIHHC

KRAYBE

NITTEK

Hey, good looking. Going my way?

WHAT SHE THOUGHT WHEN THEIR PATHS CROSSED ON THE TRAIL.

Now arrange the circled letters to form the surprise answer, as suggested by the above cartoon.

Answer here: ⬡⬡⬡⬡ A ⬡⬡⬡⬡

JUMBLE®

Unscramble these four Jumbles, one letter to each square, to form four ordinary words.

NILOG

ARROD

RINMAT

LENKEN

I thought we were going out

Ball game's on

WISE TO DO WHEN IT'S "LOVE AT FIRST SIGHT."

Now arrange the circled letters to form the surprise answer, as suggested by the above cartoon.

Answer: ◯◯◯◯ ◯◯◯◯◯

JUMBLE®

Unscramble these four Jumbles, one letter to
each square, to form four ordinary words.

ILLAC

CAUTE

COULIN

COTONY

Ya had it coming, Bart

SALOON

WHERE THE ACTOR
WAS SHOT IN
THE MOVIE.

Now arrange the circled letters to form the
surprise answer, as suggested by the above
cartoon.

Answer:

89

JUMBLE.

Unscramble these four Jumbles, one letter to each square, to form four ordinary words.

NUEQE

VIRTE

ABAANN

CLOMPY

Needs more salt

USED FOR TASTE WHEN EATING.

Now arrange the circled letters to form the surprise answer, as suggested by the above cartoon.

Print answer here: A ⭕⭕⭕⭕⭕⭕

JUMBLE

Unscramble these four Jumbles, one letter to each square, to form four ordinary words.

JUGED

CIEPE

CRAHNB

PLOATS

You'll make a cute monster

WHAT MOM DID WHEN HER SON NEEDED A HALLOWEEN COSTUME.

Now arrange the circled letters to form the surprise answer, as suggested by the above cartoon.

A: " ◯◯◯◯◯◯◯ " ◯◯◯ ◯◯

91

JUMBLE®

Unscramble these four Jumbles, one letter to each square, to form four ordinary words.

WULAF

GOMAD

REFONZ

INSOUC

LOTS OF PEOPLE MAKE THEM AT A BALL GAME.

Now arrange the circled letters to form the surprise answer, as suggested by the above cartoon.

Print your answer here:

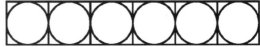

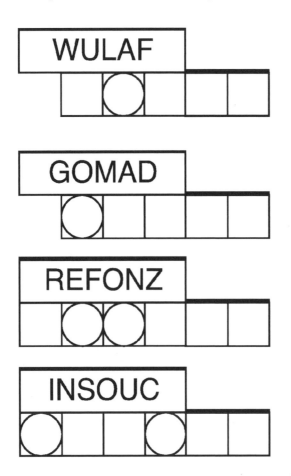

JUMBLE®

Unscramble these four Jumbles, one letter to
each square, to form four ordinary words.

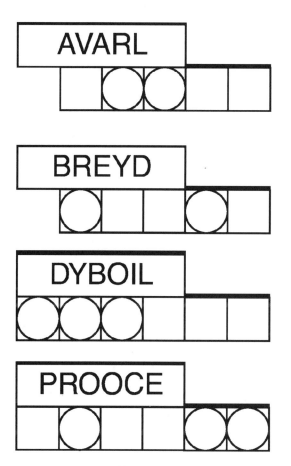

AVARL

BREYD

DYBOIL

PROOCE

We get it.
Move on

And this shows a further
breakdown of profits

SITTING THROUGH
A LENGTHY PRESENT-
ATION MADE THE
DIRECTORS A ---

Now arrange the circled letters to form the
surprise answer, as suggested by the above
cartoon.

Answer: ⬡⬡⬡⬡⬡ ⬡⬡⬡⬡⬡

JUMBLE®

Unscramble these four Jumbles, one letter to each square, to form four ordinary words.

DELOY

MOTCE

SHIMUL

ERKLAT

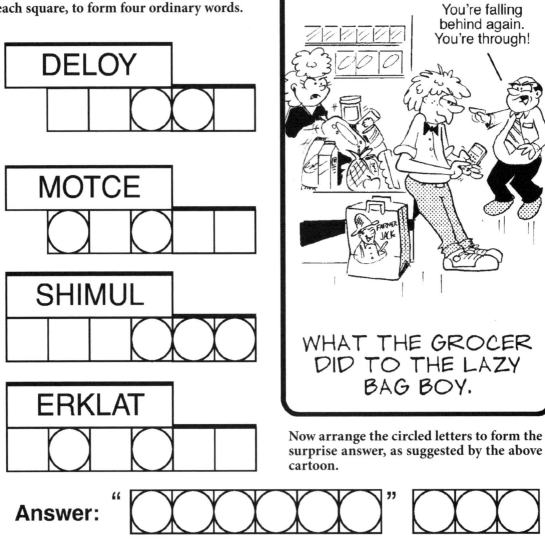

You're falling behind again. You're through!

WHAT THE GROCER DID TO THE LAZY BAG BOY.

Now arrange the circled letters to form the surprise answer, as suggested by the above cartoon.

Answer: " ⦾⦾⦾⦾⦾⦾ " ⦾⦾⦾

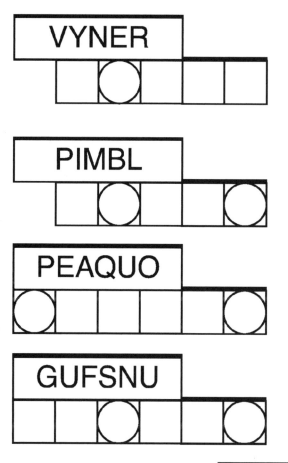

JUMBLE®

Unscramble these four Jumbles, one letter to each square, to form four ordinary words.

VYNER

PIMBL

PEAQUO

GUFSNU

Edgar, you're snoring

Sale ends tomorrow

WHEN SHE WANTED AN EXPENSIVE NEW BED, HER HUSBAND DECIDED TO - - -

Now arrange the circled letters to form the surprise answer, as suggested by the above cartoon.

Print answer here:  IT

JUMBLE®

Unscramble these four Jumbles, one letter to
each square, to form four ordinary words.

GEHIT

GALIE

WENITH

DANLUC

$1,000,000 WINNER TAKES ALL!

CLAP   CLAP   CLAP

A GOOD WAY TO
BEGIN A POKER
TOURNAMENT.

Now arrange the circled letters to form the
surprise answer, as suggested by the above
cartoon.

Answer here: ⬡⬡⬡⬡⬡ A ⬡⬡⬡⬡

PUZZLE
95

JUMBLE®

Unscramble these four Jumbles, one letter to
each square, to form four ordinary words.

ENCEP

SQUAH

PHOSUT

STEEWF

Your prints are all over the scene

WHEN THE DOORMAN WAS ARRESTED, THE DETECTIVE HAD AN...

Now arrange the circled letters to form the
surprise answer, as suggested by the above
cartoon.

A: ⃝⃝⃝⃝⃝ AND ⃝⃝⃝⃝⃝ ⃝⃝⃝⃝

97

JUMBLE®

Unscramble these four Jumbles, one letter to
each square, to form four ordinary words.

KREYJ

ROPYX

UNMEBB

CLEMUS

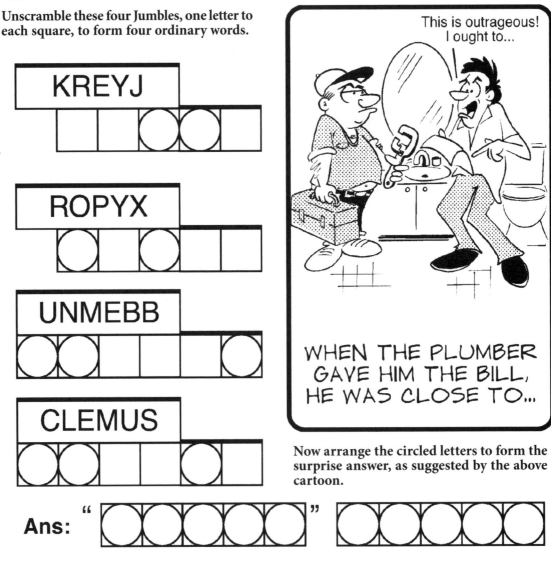

This is outrageous!
I ought to...

WHEN THE PLUMBER
GAVE HIM THE BILL,
HE WAS CLOSE TO...

Now arrange the circled letters to form the
surprise answer, as suggested by the above
cartoon.

Ans: " ◯◯◯◯◯◯ " ◯◯◯◯◯◯

97

JUMBLE®

Unscramble these four Jumbles, one letter to each square, to form four ordinary words.

KLOYE

SAGYS

MYSILF

LABEZA

I can't bring myself to shoot

WHY THE WANDERER DIDN'T ENJOY HUNTING.

Now arrange the circled letters to form the surprise answer, as suggested by the above cartoon.

Answer here: HE WAS " ⬡⬡⬡⬡⬡⬡⬡ "

JUMBLE®

Unscramble these four Jumbles, one letter to each square, to form four ordinary words.

NIGLY

TENIL

KERUBE

HIBEND

I can't wait for hotdogs

...and marshmallows

THE SCOUTS GATHERED WOOD BECAUSE THEY HAD A...

Now arrange the circled letters to form the surprise answer, as suggested by the above cartoon.

A: "☐☐☐☐☐☐☐" ☐☐☐☐

JUMBLE®

Unscramble these four Jumbles, one letter to each square, to form four ordinary words.

TEFIB

BYBOH

ENSCOD

BRILEM

WHERE THE BRAWLING HOTHEADS ENDED UP.

Now arrange the circled letters to form the surprise answer, as suggested by the above cartoon.

Ans: IN " "

JUMBLE®

Unscramble these four Jumbles, one letter to each square, to form four ordinary words.

RAMER

LIRTL

DOWPLE

ALBEFF

45 minutes to an hour

HE LEFT THE RESTAURANT WHEN THE HOSTESS SAID HE HAD A ...

Now arrange the circled letters to form the surprise answer, as suggested by the above cartoon.

A: " ⃝⃝⃝⃝ " ⃝⃝⃝⃝⃝⃝⃝⃝

102

JUMBLE®

Unscramble these four Jumbles, one letter to each square, to form four ordinary words.

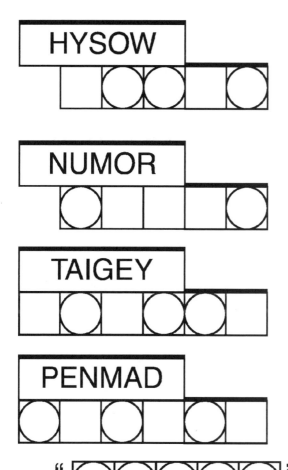

HYSOW

NUMOR

TAIGEY

PENMAD

I can't believe I won!

WHEN THE BEAUTY
QUEEN WAS
CROWNED,
IT WAS A ...

Now arrange the circled letters to form the surprise answer, as suggested by the above cartoon.

A: " ☐☐☐☐☐ " ☐☐☐☐☐☐

JUMBLE®

Unscramble these four Jumbles, one letter to
each square, to form four ordinary words.

ROFEY

MOBOL

DEXENP

HESTOO

CASUAL   This is a mess

I can't find
my size

"ROBES" ALL MIXED
UP CAN BE ...

Now arrange the circled letters to form the
surprise answer, as suggested by the above
cartoon.

Print your answer here:

JUMBLE®

Unscramble these four Jumbles, one letter to
each square, to form four ordinary words.

CITHY
〇〇 〇

ROMAR
〇〇 〇

CAPTIM
〇 〇 〇 〇

FIELDE
〇〇

Seven!
I win again

FOR A GAMBLER,
PLAYING CRAPS
CAN BE ...

Now arrange the circled letters to form the
surprise answer, as suggested by the above
cartoon.

Ans: " 〇〇〇〇 - 〇 - 〇〇〇〇 "

JUMBLE®

Unscramble these four Jumbles, one letter to each square, to form four ordinary words.

MYFIL

OEPLE

DINNAL

CHUPIC

Don't move
a muscle

WHAT THE
ACUPUNCTURIST DID
WHEN HE TREATED
THE WRESTLER.

Now arrange the circled letters to form the surprise answer, as suggested by the above cartoon.

Answer: " ⬡⬡⬡⬡⬡⬡⬡ " ⬡⬡⬡

JUMBLE®

Unscramble these four Jumbles, one letter to each square, to form four ordinary words.

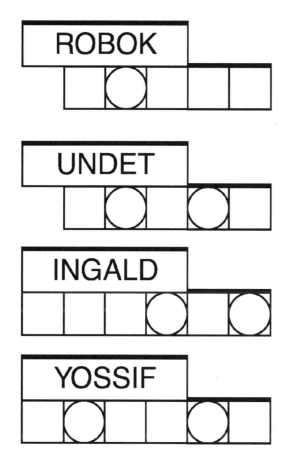

ROBOK

UNDET

INGALD

YOSSIF

You look fabulous. Only $2,500

A SUCCESSFUL DRESS DESIGNER IS GOOD WITH THIS.

Now arrange the circled letters to form the surprise answer, as suggested by the above cartoon.

Print answer here: "  "

JUMBLE®

Unscramble these four Jumbles, one letter to each square, to form four ordinary words.

YUMMG

VOLEN

PLUTIF

DUNAOL

This is the highlight of my life

WHAT THE CLIMBERS ACHIEVED WHEN THEY REACHED THE SUMMIT.

Now arrange the circled letters to form the surprise answer, as suggested by the above cartoon.

Answer: A " ⬡⬡⬡⬡⬡ " ⬡⬡⬡⬡

JUMBLE®

Unscramble these four Jumbles, one letter to
each square, to form four ordinary words.

WROCE

BOMUX

OANNEY

KIRBEC

Move this paragraph up,
and that one down

WHAT THE
REPORTER
GOT FROM THE
EDITOR.

Now arrange the circled letters to form the
surprise answer, as suggested by the above
cartoon.

Answer here:

109

JUMBLE

Unscramble these four Jumbles, one letter to each square, to form four ordinary words.

KOSMY

FETAC

ROHRRO

PAPNYS

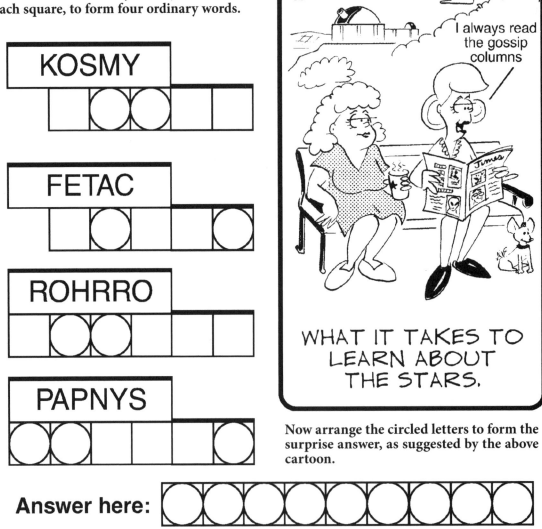

I always read the gossip columns

WHAT IT TAKES TO LEARN ABOUT THE STARS.

Now arrange the circled letters to form the surprise answer, as suggested by the above cartoon.

Answer here:

JUMBLE®

Unscramble these four Jumbles, one letter to each square, to form four ordinary words.

RACCK

YETTS

NARBER

INDUPT

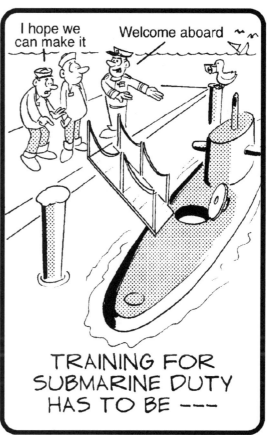

I hope we can make it

Welcome aboard

TRAINING FOR SUBMARINE DUTY HAS TO BE ---

Now arrange the circled letters to form the surprise answer, as suggested by the above cartoon.

Answer:

111

JUMBLE®

Unscramble these four Jumbles, one letter to each square, to form four ordinary words.

ITUSE

CAUDT

SHULOC

ENPOTT

You're ruining the steaks Who's going to buy this mess?

THE BUTCHER WAS LET GO BECAUSE HE ---

Now arrange the circled letters to form the surprise answer, as suggested by the above cartoon.

A:

JUMBLE®

Unscramble these four Jumbles, one letter to each square, to form four ordinary words.

YOWNS

LOCON

MOOBBA

TEAREA

It's mine for the weekend

You had it last weekend

WHEN THE PARTNERS ARGUED OVER USE OF THEIR YACHT, IT TURNED INTO ---

Now arrange the circled letters to form the surprise answer, as suggested by the above cartoon.

Answer here: A " ⬡⬡⬡⬡ " ⬡⬡⬡⬡⬡

JUMBLE®

Unscramble these four Jumbles, one letter to
each square, to form four ordinary words.

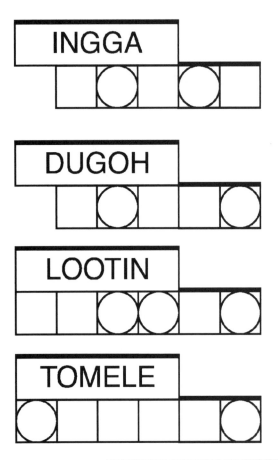

INGGA

DUGOH

LOOTIN

TOMELE

Big deal.
Like I care

WHAT THE IN-
DIFFERENT STUDENT
SAID WHEN HE GOT
A ZERO ON THE TEST.

Now arrange the circled letters to form the
surprise answer, as suggested by the above
cartoon.

Ans: " ◯◯◯◯◯◯◯◯ " ◯◯ IT

JUMBLE®

Unscramble these four Jumbles, one letter to each square, to form four ordinary words.

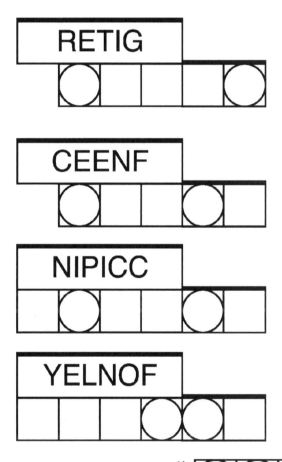

RETIG

CEENF

NIPICC

YELNOF

What comes first, me or golf?

O.K. I'm doing it

HE CHANGED THE OIL IN HIS WIFE'S CAR TO AVOID THIS.

Now arrange the circled letters to form the surprise answer, as suggested by the above cartoon.

Answer here: " ◯◯◯◯◯◯◯◯◯ "

115

JUMBLE®

Unscramble these four Jumbles, one letter to
each square, to form four ordinary words.

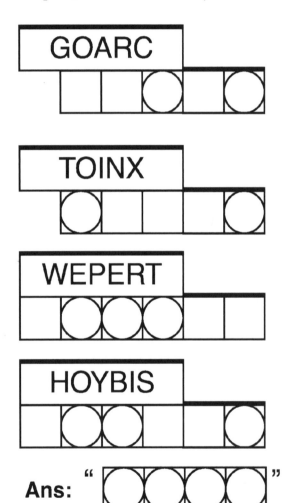

GOARC

TOINX

WEPERT

HOYBIS

He's had
dozens of hits

THE SONGWRITER
WAS IN DEMAND
BECAUSE HIS WORK
WAS ---

Now arrange the circled letters to form the
surprise answer, as suggested by the above
cartoon.

Ans: " ◯◯◯◯ " ◯◯◯◯◯◯◯

JUMBLE

Unscramble these four Jumbles, one letter to each square, to form four ordinary words.

STUMY

VANER

COTESK

VECIED

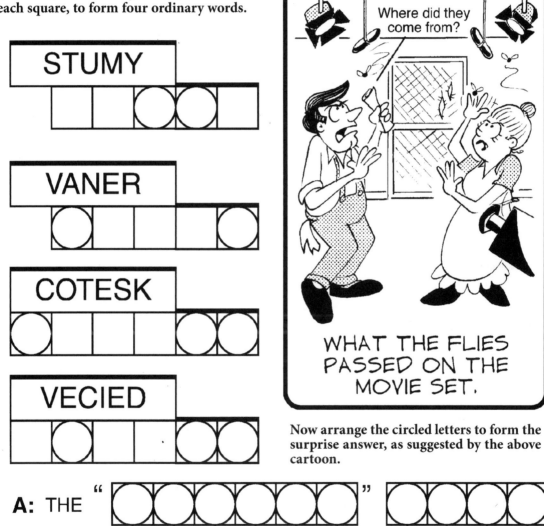

Where did they come from?

WHAT THE FLIES PASSED ON THE MOVIE SET.

Now arrange the circled letters to form the surprise answer, as suggested by the above cartoon.

A: THE " ◯◯◯◯◯◯◯ " ◯◯◯◯

JUMBLE®

Unscramble these four Jumbles, one letter to each square, to form four ordinary words.

DEESU

DANAP

PREMAT

INSORP

He makes a good living

You'll sleep like a baby

I like it

MATTRESSES CAN PROVIDE THIS.

Now arrange the circled letters to form the surprise answer, as suggested by the above cartoon.

A: ⬡⬡⬡⬡⬡⬡ OF " ⬡⬡⬡⬡⬡⬡⬡⬡ "

JUMBLE®

Unscramble these four Jumbles, one letter to each square, to form four ordinary words.

KANOE

SWENY

GOTSDY

GOTTOR

You tied it wrong

WHY THEIR BOAT FLOATED AWAY.

Now arrange the circled letters to form the surprise answer, as suggested by the above cartoon.

Answer here:

PUZZLE
118

JUMBLE®

Unscramble these four Jumbles, one letter to each square, to form four ordinary words.

ZATOP

LIEBE

GAIDOA

LEEPPO

Forget it

A GOOD WAY
TO GET IN THE
LAST WORD.

Now arrange the circled letters to form the surprise answer, as suggested by the above cartoon.

Answer here:

120

JUMBLE®

Unscramble these four Jumbles, one letter to
each square, to form four ordinary words.

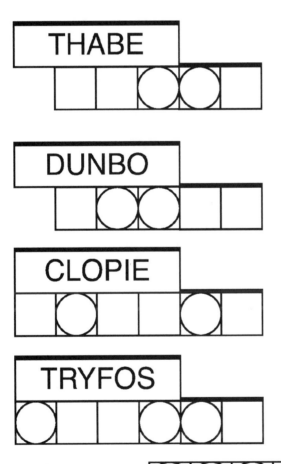

THABE

DUNBO

CLOPIE

TRYFOS

Can I have $20?

WHAT IT TAKES TO
MAKE DAD
A SOFT TOUCH.

Now arrange the circled letters to form the
surprise answer, as suggested by the above
cartoon.

Answer: A ⬡⬡⬡⬡⬡ ⬡⬡⬡⬡⬡⬡

JUMBLE®

Unscramble these four Jumbles, one letter to each square, to form four ordinary words.

IRYAH

CUNDE

CODJUN

ALFELN

They're cute

and strong

WHERE THEY WENT TO MEET HANDSOME COWBOYS.

Now arrange the circled letters to form the surprise answer, as suggested by the above cartoon.

A: TO A " ◯◯◯◯◯ " ◯◯◯◯◯◯

122

JUMBLE®

Unscramble these four Jumbles, one letter to each square, to form four ordinary words.

LUCOT

YARPT

GAYCEN

RECLAN

Look how graceful it is

WHAT THE WATCHER SAW WHEN HE SPOTTED THE SEA BIRD.

Now arrange the circled letters to form the surprise answer, as suggested by the above cartoon.

Answer here: A

JUMBLE®

Unscramble these four Jumbles, one letter to each square, to form four ordinary words.

CNARF

SINEA

SKUTEM

FLIDED

Failure to yield right of way...

I just bought it

WHAT HE ENDED UP WITH WHEN HE BUMPED THE DOCTOR'S LUXURY CAR.

Now arrange the circled letters to form the surprise answer, as suggested by the above cartoon.

A: " ◯◯◯◯ " ◯◯◯◯◯◯◯

124

JUMBLE®

Unscramble these four Jumbles, one letter to each square, to form four ordinary words.

RAWLD

HIMEC

LAWHER

GINANA

Can you fix it?

Hand me a screwdriver

WHAT THE COWBOY WHO REPAIRED THE TRUCK TURNED INTO.

Now arrange the circled letters to form the surprise answer, as suggested by the above cartoon.

Ans: A " ⬭⬭⬭⬭⬭⬭⬭ " ⬭⬭⬭⬭

JUMBLE®

Unscramble these four Jumbles, one letter to each square, to form four ordinary words.

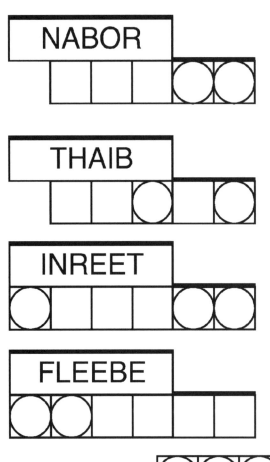

NABOR

THAIB

INREET

FLEEBE

Are you awake yet?

Everything hurts

10:30

WHEN THE BOXER LOST THE FIGHT, HE DIDN'T GET UP ---

Now arrange the circled letters to form the surprise answer, as suggested by the above cartoon.

Answer here:

126

JUMBLE®

Unscramble these four Jumbles, one letter to
each square, to form four ordinary words.

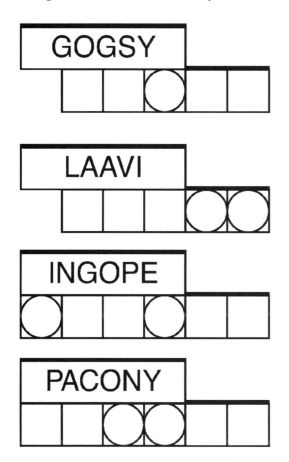

GOGSY

LAAVI

INGOPE

PACONY

Don't yell

I'm not
yelling

WHEN THEY MARRIED
IN HASTE, THEY
ENDED UP ---

Now arrange the circled letters to form the
surprise answer, as suggested by the above
cartoon.

Print answer here:

JUMBLE®

Unscramble these four Jumbles, one letter to each square, to form four ordinary words.

FEZOR

HYNIS

CEEDOD

GAYCEL

I'd rather be bungee jumping

Be careful up there

WHAT THE DAREDEVIL EXPERIENCED WHEN HE TRIMMED THE BUSHES.

Now arrange the circled letters to form the surprise answer, as suggested by the above cartoon.

Ans: ⬚⬚⬚⬚ ON THE " ⬚⬚⬚⬚⬚ "

JUMBLE®

Unscramble these four Jumbles, one letter to
each square, to form four ordinary words.

PRUPE

RUFOL

PLENOY

REVOND

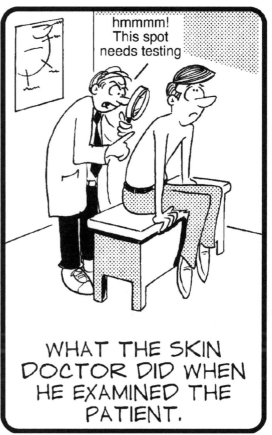

hmmmm!
This spot
needs testing

WHAT THE SKIN
DOCTOR DID WHEN
HE EXAMINED THE
PATIENT.

Now arrange the circled letters to form the
surprise answer, as suggested by the above
cartoon.

Ans: " ☐☐☐☐☐ " ☐☐☐☐ HIM

JUMBLE®

Unscramble these four Jumbles, one letter to
each square, to form four ordinary words.

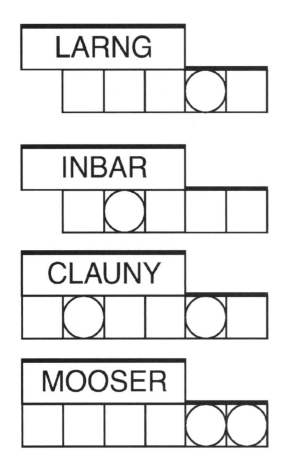

LARNG

INBAR

CLAUNY

MOOSER

!!@?!
Just when I'm
on a deadline

WHEN HIS CURSOR
FAILED, THE
REPORTER
BECAME A ----

Now arrange the circled letters to form the
surprise answer, as suggested by the above
cartoon.

Print your answer here:

JUMBLE®

Unscramble these four Jumbles, one letter to
each square, to form four ordinary words.

GOSUB

KIHCC

NATTEX

RUHLOY

That's enough,
boys

I need to
lie down

WHAT HAPPENED
WHEN THEY KEPT
DRINKING TO
THEIR HEALTH.

Now arrange the circled letters to form the
surprise answer, as suggested by the above
cartoon.

Ans: ⬚⬚⬚⬚ ⬚⬚⬚ ⬚⬚⬚⬚

JUMBLE®

Unscramble these four Jumbles, one letter to
each square, to form four ordinary words.

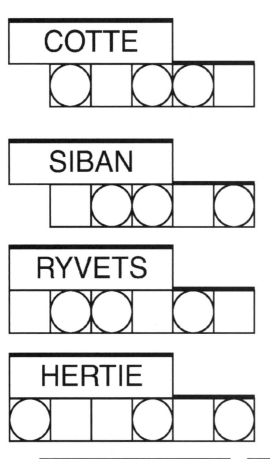

COTTE

SIBAN

RYVETS

HERTIE

What did you do?

Because I love you

WHAT IT CAN MEAN
WHEN A HUSBAND
BRINGS HOME
FLOWERS
FOR "NO REASON".

Now arrange the circled letters to form the
surprise answer, as suggested by the above
cartoon.

A: ⬭⬭⬭⬭⬭'⬭ A ⬭⬭⬭⬭⬭⬭⬭

JUMBLE®

Unscramble these four Jumbles, one letter to each square, to form four ordinary words.

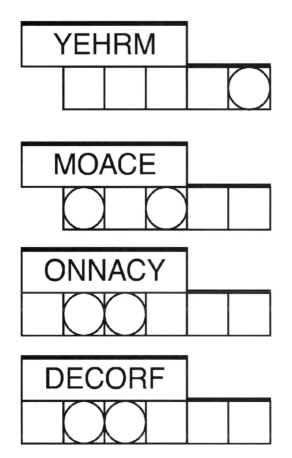

YEHRM

MOACE

ONNACY

DECORF

Today, we'll work on your abs

WHAT SHE HOPED TO DEVELOP WITH THE TRAINER.

Now arrange the circled letters to form the surprise answer, as suggested by the above cartoon.

Print answer here: A ⬡⬡⬡⬡⬡⬡⬡

JUMBLE®

Unscramble these four Jumbles, one letter to each square, to form four ordinary words.

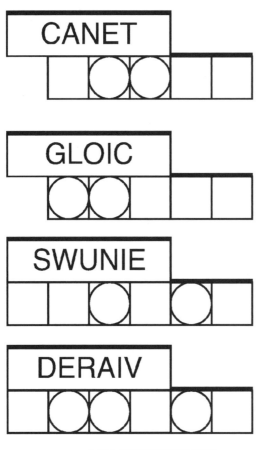

CANET

GLOIC

SWUNIE

DERAIV

He's tough to deal with

WHY THE BANKER DIDN'T HAVE MANY FRIENDS

Now arrange the circled letters to form the surprise answer, as suggested by the above cartoon.

A: HE ◯◯◯ A " ◯◯◯◯◯◯◯ "

PUZZLE
133

JUMBLE®

Unscramble these four Jumbles, one letter to each square, to form four ordinary words.

HECKE

SINUM

GILOOG

THYFOR

Whoo! I put in daisies, marigolds, zinnias and ...

WHAT THE TIRED GARDENER PLANTED.

Now arrange the circled letters to form the surprise answer, as suggested by the above cartoon.

Print answer here:

135

JUMBLE®

Unscramble these four Jumbles, one letter to each square, to form four ordinary words.

TREXE

BOTOR

ROTTET

URREBB

He learned how
to bluff

I stole
that hand

WHEN THE GAMBLER
TOOK POKER
LESSONS, HE
BECAME A ---

Now arrange the circled letters to form the surprise answer, as suggested by the above cartoon.

A:

JUMBLE®

Unscramble these four Jumbles, one letter to each square, to form four ordinary words.

ECKER

RODAH

FLUBEM

CALAPA

How do you like my new recipe?

It seems underdone

WHEN THE CHEF TRIED A NEW DISH, THE DINERS SAID IT WAS ---

Now arrange the circled letters to form the surprise answer, as suggested by the above cartoon.

Answer here:

137

JUMBLE®

Unscramble these four Jumbles, one letter to each square, to form four ordinary words.

BOAVE

HIRAC

MARFFI

LOFUND

I'm late for my meeting

...and if I'm elected...

VOTE

WHAT THE EXECUTIVE AND POLITICIAN HAD IN COMMON.

Now arrange the circled letters to form the surprise answer, as suggested by the above cartoon.

A:

138

JUMBLE®

Unscramble these four Jumbles, one letter to each square, to form four ordinary words.

NOYGA

DELAL

LAPEAT

DRYBOW

$5,000 REWARD

21766

HOW THE LONELY BANK ROBBER FELT WHEN HE SAW HIS POSTER.

Now arrange the circled letters to form the surprise answer, as suggested by the above cartoon.

Print your answer here:

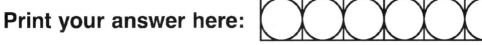

JUMBLE ®

Unscramble these four Jumbles, one letter to each square, to form four ordinary words.

ADGEL

BYASS

TELKIN

KNIBAG

I'm out of chips

Dinner's on you

WHAT THE POKER GROUP PLAYED FOR.

Now arrange the circled letters to form the surprise answer, as suggested by the above cartoon.

Answer here:

JUMBLE®

Unscramble these four Jumbles, one letter to each square, to form four ordinary words.

SULPH

POURC

ORREBB

QUETEA

First I'll have my coffee, then I'll read the paper and then ...

HOW LONG DID IT TAKE THE COMMUTER TO GET TO WORK?

Now arrange the circled letters to form the surprise answer, as suggested by the above cartoon.

Answer: ⬭⬭⬭⬭⬭ AN ⬭⬭⬭⬭

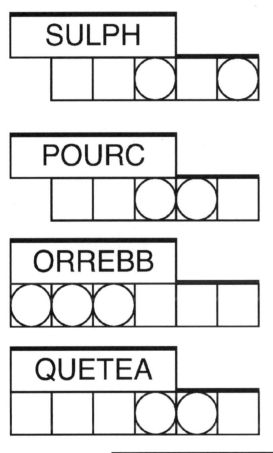

JUMBLE®

Unscramble these four Jumbles, one letter to each square, to form four ordinary words.

LUSKK

KAWTE

YARROS

WARBOR

I'll replace the battery, spring and clean it up

WHAT A WATCH REPAIRER DOES.

Now arrange the circled letters to form the surprise answer, as suggested by the above cartoon.

Ans: ⬡⬡⬡⬡⬡ THE ⬡⬡⬡⬡⬡

JUMBLE®

Unscramble these four Jumbles, one letter to
each square, to form four ordinary words.

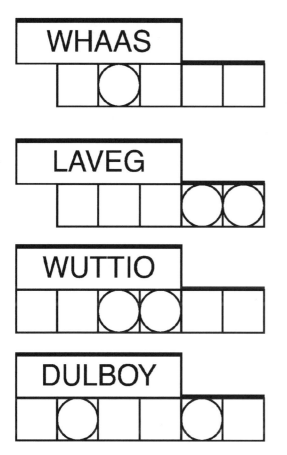

WHAAS

LAVEG

WUTTIO

DULBOY

I adore both of
them

HE TURNED OUT
TO BE A BIGAMIST
BECAUSE
HE LOVED ---

Now arrange the circled letters to form the
surprise answer, as suggested by the above
cartoon.

Print answer here:

PUZZLE
142

JUMBLE®

Unscramble these four Jumbles, one letter to each square, to form four ordinary words.

DAIDE

POUMI

YINCLE

NAHZIG

He's good

Wonderful depth

WHAT THE STREET ARTIST DREW.

Now arrange the circled letters to form the surprise answer, as suggested by the above cartoon.

Answer here: AN ◯◯◯◯◯◯◯◯◯

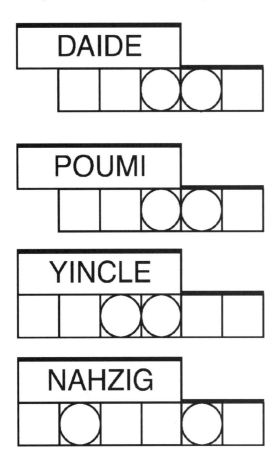

144

JUMBLE®

Unscramble these four Jumbles, one letter to each square, to form four ordinary words.

FUTLE

YATHS

WEREVS

MARDRO

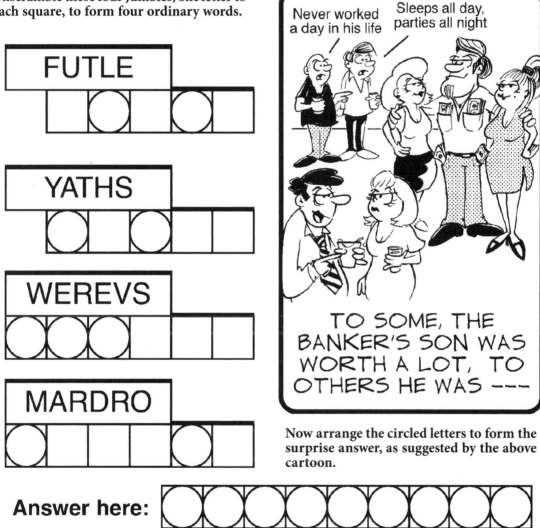

Never worked a day in his life

Sleeps all day, parties all night

TO SOME, THE BANKER'S SON WAS WORTH A LOT, TO OTHERS HE WAS ---

Now arrange the circled letters to form the surprise answer, as suggested by the above cartoon.

Answer here:

JUMBLE®

Unscramble these four Jumbles, one letter to
each square, to form four ordinary words.

DOREL

GOBEF

POOSUR

GROOFT

It's like walking
on marshmallows

WHAT A
COMFORTABLE
SHOE CAN BE.

Now arrange the circled letters to form the
surprise answer, as suggested by the above
cartoon.

A: ☐☐☐☐☐ ☐☐☐ THE ☐☐☐☐

JUMBLE®

Unscramble these four Jumbles, one letter to
each square, to form four ordinary words.

WEHIN

HOCAP

TROIMP

SUFOAM

My deadline is
coming up

Mine too!

WHEN THEY RACED
TO DEVELOP THE
NEWS PICTURES,
IT WAS A ---

Now arrange the circled letters to form the
surprise answer, as suggested by the above
cartoon.

A: ⬡⬡⬡⬡⬡ " ⬡⬡⬡⬡⬡⬡⬡ "

147

JUMBLE

Unscramble these four Jumbles, one letter to each square, to form four ordinary words.

LICCO

BLYUL

HARGIS

PICTES

This is your first lesson

WATER DUNES C

WHAT THE RETIREE NEEDED WHEN HE DECIDED TO TAKE UP GOLF.

Now arrange the circled letters to form the surprise answer, as suggested by the above cartoon.

Print answer here: A " ◯◯◯◯◯◯ "

JUMBLE®

Unscramble these four Jumbles, one letter to each square, to form four ordinary words.

HESEP

LUTEL

VHIALS

INLOPP

THE SHOP OWNER'S DONUT DISCOUNT AMOUNTED TO ----

Now arrange the circled letters to form the surprise answer, as suggested by the above cartoon.

Answer here: " ◯◯◯◯ " ◯◯◯◯

JUMBLE®

Unscramble these four Jumbles, one letter to each square, to form four ordinary words.

TYTUP

INVEG

NESIPP

SNIBAH

I'll need a big loan, but this is a good location

FOR SALE

WHAT THE EYE DOCTOR REQUIRED FOR HIS NEW OFFICE BUILDING.

Now arrange the circled letters to form the surprise answer, as suggested by the above cartoon.

Answer: A ⭕⭕⭕⭕⭕ ⭕⭕⭕⭕

JUMBLE®

Unscramble these four Jumbles, one letter to each square, to form four ordinary words.

NEVET

DAAMM

DRATOW

CONIVE

I'm hanging ten

Let's ride this baby

WHAT THE MOBSTERS EXPERIENCED WHEN THEY WENT SURFING.

Now arrange the circled letters to form the surprise answer, as suggested by the above cartoon.

Ans: A ⭕⭕⭕⭕⭕ " ⭕⭕⭕⭕ "

JUMBLE®

Unscramble these four Jumbles, one letter to
each square, to form four ordinary words.

EKQUA

NOWNK

CENNAD

LAUTAC

Quiet!
I'll feed
you later.

WHEN THE NOISY PET
DUCK WOKE UP THE
FARMBOY,
IT WAS THE ---

Now arrange the circled letters to form the
surprise answer, as suggested by the above
cartoon.

Ans: " ⬡⬡⬡⬡⬡ " OF ⬡⬡⬡⬡

JUMBLE®

Unscramble these four Jumbles, one letter to each square, to form four ordinary words.

MOBIL

EXOID

SKROHE

MIOGES

She's brilliant

I found a new strain

THIS HELPED THE PRETTY BIOLOGIST GET AHEAD.

Now arrange the circled letters to form the surprise answer, as suggested by the above cartoon.

A: HER ⬚⬚⬚⬚ " ⬚⬚⬚⬚⬚ "

153

JUMBLE®

Unscramble these four Jumbles, one letter to each square, to form four ordinary words.

MAORA

GWEED

RIMSEY

ECPPIT

This book will take you far away

WHAT THE CONVICT SOUGHT AT THE PRISON LIBRARY.

Now arrange the circled letters to form the surprise answer, as suggested by the above cartoon.

A: A ◯◯◯ TO "◯◯◯◯◯◯"

JUMBLE®

Unscramble these four Jumbles, one letter to
each square, to form four ordinary words.

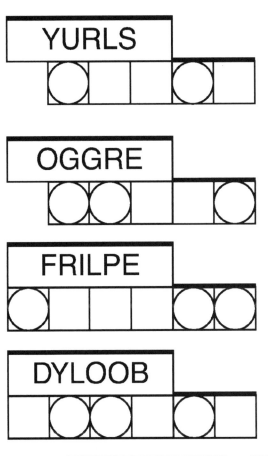

YURLS

OGGRE

FRILPE

DYLOOB

Where did she come from?

THE YOUNG WITCH
JOINED THE BEE CON-
TESTANTS BECAUSE
SHE WAS ---

Now arrange the circled letters to form the
surprise answer, as suggested by the above
cartoon.

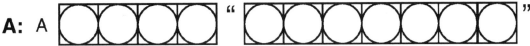

A: A ⬡⬡⬡⬡ " ⬡⬡⬡⬡⬡⬡⬡ "

155

JUMBLE®

Unscramble these four Jumbles, one letter to
each square, to form four ordinary words.

REMEG

NEWIT

MELFYS

INJEYT

C'mon.
I'll race you

HOW THE TEENS GOT
ALONG WHEN THEY
MET AT THE POOL.

Now arrange the circled letters to form the
surprise answer, as suggested by the above
cartoon.

Ans: " ◯◯◯◯◯◯◯◯◯◯◯ "

JUMBLE®

Unscramble these four Jumbles, one letter to each square, to form four ordinary words.

UPDYM

GALEL

STEACK

ZULZEG

What have I done?

WHAT THE ROWER SUFFERED WHEN HIS BOAT HIT THE PIER.

Now arrange the circled letters to form the surprise answer, as suggested by the above cartoon.

Ans:

JUMBLE®

Unscramble these four Jumbles, one letter to
each square, to form four ordinary words.

EGGAU

CILRY

TUIFLE

HARTHS

EEK! Lola,
What did you
do to yourself?

WHEN THE BEAUTY
QUEEN BECAME A WITCH
FOR HALLOWEEN,
SHE WAS A ---

Now arrange the circled letters to form the
surprise answer, as suggested by the above
cartoon.

Print answer here: " ◯◯◯◯◯◯ "

JUMBLE®

Unscramble these four Jumbles, one letter to
each square, to form four ordinary words.

LAROF

WORNC

UNEAVE

YELMOP

It's past quitting time

Let's finish the room

THE PAPER HANGERS
WORKED LATE
BECAUSE THEY ---

Now arrange the circled letters to form the
surprise answer, as suggested by the above
cartoon.

Answer: ⬭⬭⬭⬭ ON A " ⬭⬭⬭⬭⬭ "

159

JUMBLE®

Unscramble these four Jumbles, one letter to each square, to form four ordinary words.

CHALT

MYTEP

DELDUP

ENCOAB

I kept it warm for you, dear

WHAT THE SECOND BASE UMPIRE GOT AFTER THE GAME.

Now arrange the circled letters to form the surprise answer, as suggested by the above cartoon.

Answer: " "

JUMBLE®

Unscramble these four Jumbles, one letter to
each square, to form four ordinary words.

LUCCK

ELLEB

KIALLA

RUZZEB

I'm sore all over

THE BOXER ENTERED
THE RING WEARING
RED AND WHITE
AND LEFT ---

Now arrange the circled letters to form the
surprise answer, as suggested by the above
cartoon.

Answer:  AND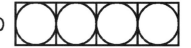

161

JUMBLE

Unscramble these four Jumbles, one letter to each square, to form four ordinary words.

RHOBA

ROBIT

SAKMAD

FIMSIT

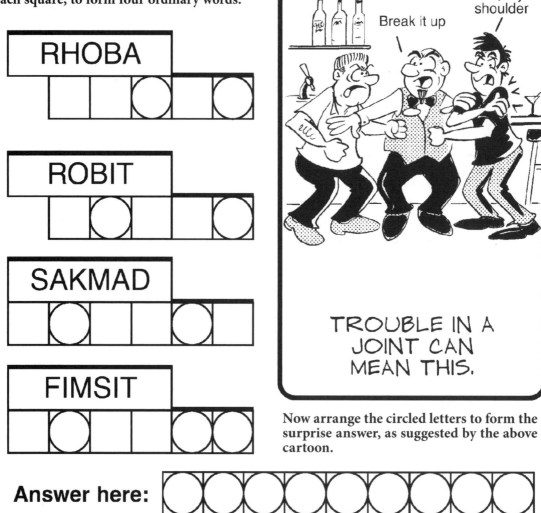

Break it up

Oh, my shoulder

TROUBLE IN A JOINT CAN MEAN THIS.

Now arrange the circled letters to form the surprise answer, as suggested by the above cartoon.

Answer here:

162

JUMBLE®
Jitterbug

Challenger
Puzzles

JUMBLE®

Unscramble these six Jumbles, one letter to each square, to form six ordinary words.

BLOIME

GRAUSY

SUMMUE

NALDAV

ADBALL

MYLAHN

This is old, Grandma

I like the pictures

1988

MARCH
1 2 3 4 5

3/30

THIS IS TRUE
NO MATTER HOW
LONG A CALENDAR
IS KEPT.

Now arrange the circled letters to form the surprise answer, as suggested by the above cartoon.

Print answer here

ITS ⬭⬭⬭⬭ ARE "⬭⬭⬭⬭⬭⬭⬭⬭"

JUMBLE®

Unscramble these six Jumbles, one letter to
each square, to form six ordinary words.

NIPURT

SETTAL

GREESY

PLYENT

GINRAD

TEMNEC

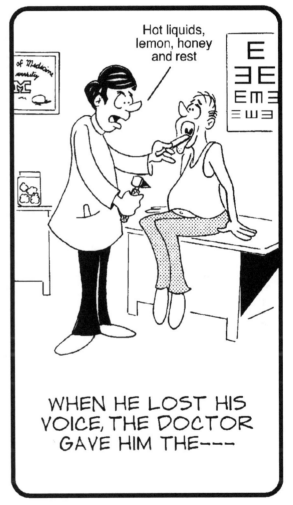

Hot liquids,
lemon, honey
and rest

WHEN HE LOST HIS
VOICE, THE DOCTOR
GAVE HIM THE---

Now arrange the circled letters to form the
surprise answer, as suggested by the above
cartoon.

Print answer here

165

JUMBLE®

Unscramble these six Jumbles, one letter to each square, to form six ordinary words.

LEFTLI

TRUXAS

INKELT

LUZZEG

YURFIP

YERTOP

This is so comfy.
I could take
a nap

WHEN THE MODEL
POSED IN THE EASY
CHAIR, SHE WAS ---

Now arrange the circled letters to form the surprise answer, as suggested by the above cartoon.

Print answer here

" "

JUMBLE®

Unscramble these six Jumbles, one letter to each square, to form six ordinary words.

NISSIT

DELAUF

DREEME

GERUDD

DOYLOB

BRUZZE

I took out a loan to keep them fed

WHEN THE RACE HORSES KEPT LOSING, THEIR OWNER WAS ---

Now arrange the circled letters to form the surprise answer, as suggested by the above cartoon.

Print answer here

" ⬡⬡⬡⬡⬡⬡⬡ " WITH ⬡⬡⬡⬡

167

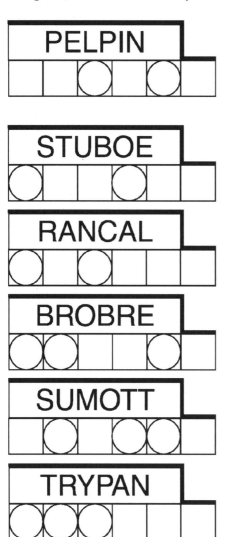

JUMBLE

Unscramble these six Jumbles, one letter to each square, to form six ordinary words.

PELPIN

STUBOE

RANCAL

BROBRE

SUMOTT

TRYPAN

I'll take it. How 'bout dinner tonight?

WHAT THE BUYER OFFERED WHEN THE SALESWOMAN SHOWED HIM A TIE

Now arrange the circled letters to form the surprise answer, as suggested by the above cartoon.

Print answer here

A " ◯◯◯◯◯◯◯◯ " ◯◯◯◯◯◯◯◯◯

JUMBLE®

Unscramble these six Jumbles, one letter to each square, to form six ordinary words.

CYMALL

INGOHM

BLACOT

LESFAT

DISNAL

EHLTMA

CLASS of 2009

Mostly B's. The tutor really helped

WHAT IT TOOK TO GET HIS SON THROUGH COLLEGE

Now arrange the circled letters to form the surprise answer, as suggested by the above cartoon.

Print answer here

⬡⬡⬡⬡⬡⬡ ⬡⬡⬡ **HE** ⬡⬡⬡

169

JUMBLE®

Unscramble these six Jumbles, one letter to each square, to form six ordinary words.

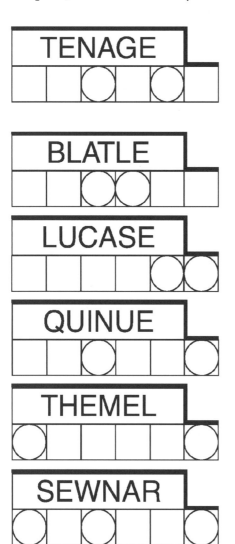

TENAGE

BLATLE

LUCASE

QUINUE

THEMEL

SEWNAR

Time to go shopping

WHEN HE GOT HOLES IN HIS SOCKS, HE SAID THEY WERE ON ---

Now arrange the circled letters to form the surprise answer, as suggested by the above cartoon.

Print answer here

170

JUMBLE®

Unscramble these six Jumbles, one letter to
each square, to form six ordinary words.

NERRED

CLAJAK

ETEELY

TELKAN

REPACT

DELBEH

Not
bad

Good
evening,
officer

WHAT THE MUSICIAN
DID WHEN HE
BECAME A POLICEMAN.

Now arrange the circled letters to form the
surprise answer, as suggested by the above
cartoon.

Print answer here

171

JUMBLE®

Unscramble these six Jumbles, one letter to each square, to form six ordinary words.

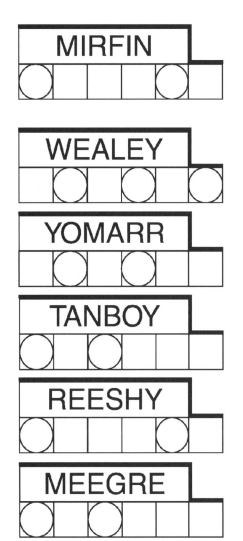

MIRFIN

WEALEY

YOMARR

TANBOY

REESHY

MEEGRE

Soon you'll have a scarf

Over, then under, then what?

WHAT SOME MEN CAN END UP KNITTING.

Now arrange the circled letters to form the surprise answer, as suggested by the above cartoon.

Print answer here

172

JUMBLE®

Unscramble these six Jumbles, one letter to
each square, to form six ordinary words.

BLAMCY

BARNEY

REEFIC

CARPHE

SLYMIA

ENCAME

Careful
where
you step

OW!

THESE CAN MAKE
YOUR FEET HURT
WHEN VISITING
ANCIENT RUINS.

Now arrange the circled letters to form the
surprise answer, as suggested by the above
cartoon.

Print answer here

173

JUMBLE®

Unscramble these six Jumbles, one letter to
each square, to form six ordinary words.

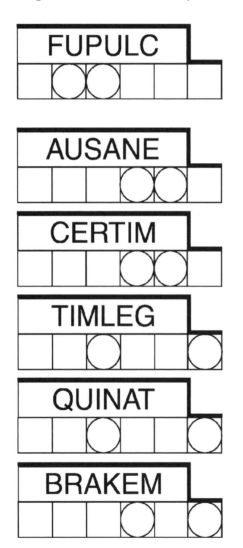

FUPULC

AUSANE

CERTIM

TIMLEG

QUINAT

BRAKEM

After you,
my dear

Thank you,
sweetheart

WHEN THE COUPLE
RECONCILED, THEY
SAID THE MARRIAGE
COUNSELOR WAS A ---

Now arrange the circled letters to form the
surprise answer, as suggested by the above
cartoon.

Print answer here

" ⬡⬡⬡⬡⬡⬡ " ⬡⬡⬡⬡⬡⬡

174

JUMBLE®

Unscramble these six Jumbles, one letter to
each square, to form six ordinary words.

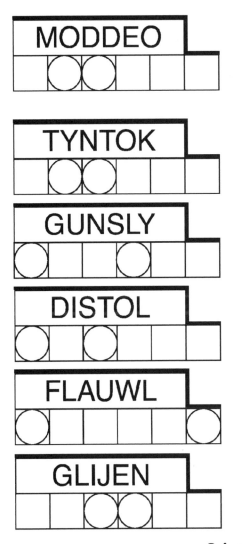

MODDEO

TYNTOK

GUNSLY

DISTOL

FLAUWL

GLIJEN

A3

I'll miss you

Hurry, your
plane is
leaving

THEIR EXTENDED
GOOD-BYE TURNED
INTO A ---

Now arrange the circled letters to form the
surprise answer, as suggested by the above
cartoon.

Print answer here

⬚⬚ ⬚⬚⬚⬚ " ⬚⬚ - ⬚⬚⬚⬚ "

JUMBLE®

Unscramble these six Jumbles, one letter to
each square, to form six ordinary words.

TRUFUE

ENGOUL

YATUBE

FLADGY

SENFUI

RUBBUS

Hurry there are
more shops
ahead

WHAT BUSY LADIES
DID DURING THE
VICTORIAN ERA.

Now arrange the circled letters to form the
surprise answer, as suggested by the above
cartoon.

Print answer here

176

PUZZLE
174

JUMBLE®

Unscramble these six Jumbles, one letter to each square, to form six ordinary words.

COLOTE

INLOVI

CARILA

DHINER

BAYTER

GELIGG

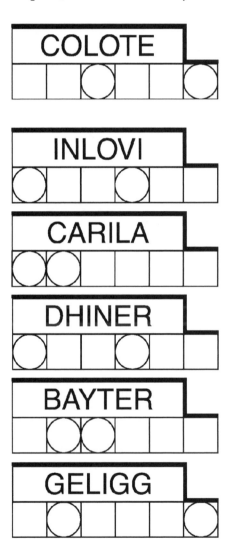

If he's not here in two minutes, the wedding's off

WHEN THE GROOM WAS LATE, THE BRIDE MADE A----

Now arrange the circled letters to form the surprise answer, as suggested by the above cartoon.

Print answer here

" ◯◯◯◯◯◯ " ◯◯◯◯◯◯

177

JUMBLE®

Unscramble these six Jumbles, one letter to each square, to form six ordinary words.

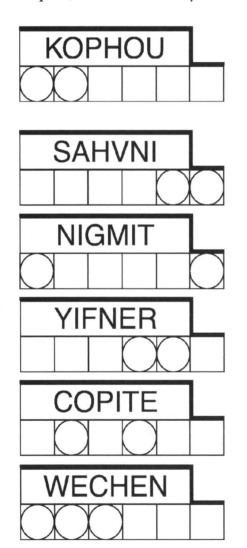

KOPHOU

SAHVNI

NIGMIT

YIFNER

COPITE

WECHEN

This is spooky

WHAT THE GUARD SAID WHEN HE APPROACHED THE HAUNTED HOUSE.

Now arrange the circled letters to form the surprise answer, as suggested by the above cartoon.

Print answer here

" ___ ' _____ ' _____ ? "

JUMBLE®

Unscramble these six Jumbles, one letter to each square, to form six ordinary words.

ROOLIE

SOUTID

PHILSO

WHYTOR

REESHA

GROUME

I'm down to my last chips

WEARING A TIE TO A FANCY CASINO DOESN'T MEAN YOU WON'T DO THIS.

Now arrange the circled letters to form the surprise answer, as suggested by the above cartoon.

Print answer here

JUMBLE®

Unscramble these six Jumbles, one letter to each square, to form six ordinary words.

RIFUGE

TICPED

LEWFOL

LEESAW

UDDEGI

LOONED

WHAT THE SWIMMERS DID TO WIN THE RELAY RACE.

Now arrange the circled letters to form the surprise answer, as suggested by the above cartoon.

Print answer here

" ◯◯◯◯◯◯ " THEIR ◯◯◯◯◯◯◯◯

180

JUMBLE®

Unscramble these six Jumbles, one letter to each square, to form six ordinary words.

YURJIN

DRAFTI

TAISER

DRAIMY

TERVID

ROVEXT

That's our new professor

He's an expert on the past

THE HISTORIAN RETURNED TO HIS ALMA MATER BECAUSE HE WAS A---

Now arrange the circled letters to form the surprise answer, as suggested by the above cartoon.

Print answer here

181

JUMBLE®

Unscramble these six Jumbles, one letter to each square, to form six ordinary words.

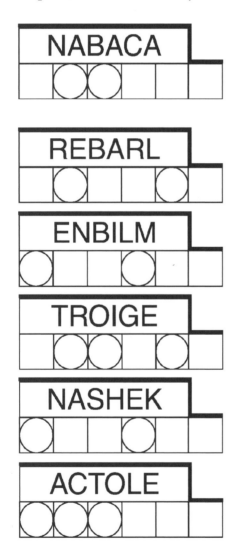

NABACA

REBARL

ENBILM

TROIGE

NASHEK

ACTOLE

I'll pay Big Tony $5,000 today and hold off on Tough Tom until next week

SPORTS

DIFFICULT FOR A BIG-TIME BETTOR TO DO.

Now arrange the circled letters to form the surprise answer, as suggested by the above cartoon.

Print answer here

◯◯◯◯◯◯◯ HIS ◯◯◯◯◯◯◯◯

JUMBLE®

Unscramble these six Jumbles, one letter to each square, to form six ordinary words.

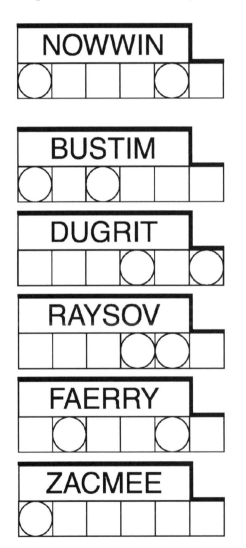

NOWWIN

BUSTIM

DUGRIT

RAYSOV

FAERRY

ZACMEE

WHEN THE PUB CRAWLER HEARD THE DRINKING SONG, IT WAS ---

Now arrange the circled letters to form the surprise answer, as suggested by the above cartoon.

Print answer here

○○○○○ FOR A ○○○ "○○○○○"

183

Answers

1. **Jumbles:** FUSSY CRUSH KISMET JACKET
   Answer: Why the boxer joined the soccer team —
   JUST FOR "KICKS"

2. **Jumbles:** BAKED USURP CUDDLE CANDID
   Answer: Where ideals can come from — LADIES

3. **Jumbles:** TEMPO UNWED RADISH FACADE
   Answer: The students admired the archaeologist because he
   was — DOWN TO EARTH

4. **Jumbles:** WEARY EPOCH OUTFIT RAREFY
   Answer: When the charter pilot's son took over the business,
   it became an — HEIR FORCE

5. **Jumbles:** NIPPY LOOSE BEYOND DEFACE
   Answer: What air travelers get, even in first class —
   "PLANE" FOOD

6. **Jumbles:** JETTY MOUSE GAMBOL TYPHUS
   Answer: In a bar, sitting down can result in — BOTTOMS UP

7. **Jumbles:** LIBEL PIKER UNCURL HANDLE
   Answer: One result of being riled — IDLER

8. **Jumbles:** RAJAH BRIBE EFFACE INDIGO
   Answer: A busy blacksmith will do this — "FORGE" AHEAD

9. **Jumbles:** FEINT AMITY WIZARD SMILES
   Answer: A middle-age paunch can be a — "WAIST" OF TIME

10. **Jumbles:** PEONY FAMED BRIDLE EASILY
    Answer: Why the young ball player didn't have a steady
    girlfriend — HE PLAYED THE "FIELD"

11. **Jumbles:** DICED LIGHT FACIAL GIBLET
    Answer: Giving Junior a heap of educational toys made him
    a — "GIFTED" CHILD

12. **Jumbles:** ABASH DRAMA SNITCH ABSORB
    Answer: The secretary concentrated on this —
    THE SHORT HAND

13. **Jumbles:** VITAL IVORY NIBBLE SLOGAN
    Answer: Watching an ironworker high on a skyscraper can
    be — "RIVETING"

14. **Jumbles:** EXUDE LIMIT CHARGE UNEASY
    Answer: When the mechanic installed the new muffler,
    it was — "EXHAUSTING"

15. **Jumbles:** IGLOO KNEEL UPWARD FLUNKY
    Answer: When she changed her hair color, it was —
    TO "DYE" FOR

16. **Jumbles:** TRULY SOUSE IMMUNE HEALTH
    Answer: What the businessmen read before breakfast —
    THE MENU

17. **Jumbles:** BATCH PRONE CHERUB MEASLY
    Answer: What the teen-agers turned into after a dip in the
    ocean — BEACH COMBERS

18. **Jumbles:** DUNCE OZONE FRIEZE BLUISH
    Answer: When the cats performed for the animal trainer, he
    was — "LIONIZED"

19. **Jumbles:** SAVOR SWISH GLANCE MAMMAL
    Answer: When the artist was asked what was behind the
    painting, he said it — WAS A CANVAS

20. **Jumbles:** NOTCH ADULT GOITER SAVORY
    Answer: When the ballet star helped her dancemate,
    she did a — GOOD "TURN"

21. **Jumbles:** GRAVE OBESE CRABBY SUBMIT
    Answer: When vandals used spray paint on the steps, police
    said it was — A STAIR "CASE"

22. **Jumbles:** TWILL PARCH SECEDE ZEALOT
    Answer: Why the young king refused to wear a crown —
    IT WAS OLD "HAT"

23. **Jumbles:** ABIDE SYNOD ABDUCT GUNNER
    Answer: When Mom sewed the hole in his sock, she
    considered it a — "DARN" NUISANCE

24. **Jumbles:** GAWKY CLUCK THROAT TRUANT
    Answer: When the phony trapeze artist fell into the net, he
    was — CAUGHT IN THE "ACT"

25. **Jumbles:** GULCH PANIC SPRUCE BICEPS
    Answer: When the crew lined up for haircuts, the submarine
    became — A "CLIPPER" SHIP

26. **Jumbles:** UNCAP GLORY CHISEL BOTTLE
    Answer: What the tallest player did when the team stayed in
    a hotel — SLEPT "LONGER"

27. **Jumbles:** TRUTH PLAIT FUSION GRISLY
    Answer: What happened when his grip was lost —
    HE LOST HIS "GRIP"

28. **Jumbles:** IRONY WEIGH WHINNY SUNDAE
    Answer: She was attracted to the card shark because
    he had — "WINNING" WAYS

29. **Jumbles:** PERKY LATHE RADIAL PESTLE
    Answer: In the old west, a six-shooter was an —
    EARLY "SETTLER"

30. **Jumbles:** LEAVE POKED FETISH MARTYR
    Answer: She dumped her boyfriend because she wanted a
    future and he — HAD A PAST

31. **Jumbles:** PRIOR FINIS INFANT MINGLE
    Answer: Why the balloons went up — "INFLATION"

32. **Jumbles:** LISLE ADMIT CLOTHE KNIGHT
    Answer: Being loose with money can lead to this —
    "TIGHT" TIMES

33. **Jumbles:** ENSUE FLAKE ADJOIN VERIFY
    Answer: The referee thought the defensive lineman was —
    OFFENSIVE

34. **Jumbles:** GROOM DRYLY COUPON INVENT
    Answer: Easy to become when modeling fur coats —
    A "COVER" GIRL

35. **Jumbles:** MOUND BLESS FOSSIL WHEEZE
    Answer: When the doughnut maker bought out his partner,
    he got the — "HOLE" BUSINESS

36. **Jumbles:** QUILT METAL GIGOLO INNING
    Answer: How the electrician described the preacher's
    sermon — "ILLUMINATING"

37. **Jumbles:** VOCAL GRIMY LICHEN SHOULD
    Answer: The cheerleader said her beau, the sprinter, was —
    "DASHING"

38. **Jumbles:** BOOTY HAVEN OUTLAW OXYGEN
    Answer: Where he went when he stopped drinking —
    ON THE WAGON

39. **Jumbles:** NIECE VALVE IMPEDE SLEIGH
    Answer: The escapee broke into the tannery because it was
    a — "HIDING" PLACE

40. **Jumbles:** SIXTY LOONY THEORY SHAKEN
    Answer: What the boxer did when his girlfriend's little
    brother appeared — TOOK IT ON THE SHIN

41. **Jumbles:** TWICE FLOOD WALLOP CANYON
    Answer: What the tenant got when he rented the basement
    apartment — THE "LOW-DOWN"

42. **Jumbles:** SNACK ABYSS OUTCRY VIABLE
    Answer: A good way to improve the view at a football
    game — BINOCULARS

43. **Jumbles:** BLANK JOINT GRUBBY COUGAR
    Answer: Filling the gas tank these days can leave you —
    "BURNING"

44. **Jumbles:** AZURE SHYLY FURROW FAUCET
    Answer: When the manager kept changing pitchers, the
    southpaw — WAS "LEFT"

45. **Jumbles:** FATAL JADED NICELY CAVORT
    Answer: When her fiancé got hot under the collar, she ended
    up with — COLD FEET

46. **Jumbles:** POACH TASTY SADIST MISHAP
    Answer: The convict enjoyed sitting in the sun because he
    had a — "SHADY" PAST

47. **Jumbles:** ROBOT QUEST ZITHER CATNIP
    Answer: When the ex-strikeout king sold cars, he used his —
    BEST "PITCH"

48. **Jumbles:** EXERT VOUCH WEEVIL NEWEST
Answer: What the bath shop did when business soured —
THREW IN THE TOWEL

49. **Jumbles:** VIXEN AGONY MODIFY BEFALL
Answer: For a traffic court judge, it's always a — "FINE" DAY

50. **Jumbles:** BEFOG DOUBT CRAYON BYGONE
Answer: What he bid at the auction — GOOD BYE

51. **Jumbles:** TAKEN PLUME COLUMN INDUCT
Answer: The carpenter fired his helper because he —
COULDN'T "CUT" IT

52. **Jumbles:** STUNG WHISK AUTUMN IMPORT
Answer: When the cleaner ruined the lawyer's outfit, he
faced a — SUIT SUIT

53. **Jumbles:** ABOVE TOOTH PLURAL TARTAR
Answer: Easy to get without a lot of trouble —
A LOT OF TROUBLE

54. **Jumbles:** CASTE QUAKE STICKY CENSUS
Answer: When the concert pianist performed, he exhibited
his — "KEYS" TO SUCCESS

55. **Jumbles:** MADAM GAUGE KERNEL RUBBER
Answer: Although she was stuck-up, her looks made him —
"UNGLUED"

56. **Jumbles:** GROIN EVENT DENTAL HERALD
Answer: When the doctor didn't charge him, the young
patient was — "TREATED"

57. **Jumbles:** DUMPY OPIUM HALLOW DONKEY
Answer: What the schoolboys did when they met the
basketball star — LOOKED "UP" TO HIM

58. **Jumbles:** KNELL ACRID WALNUT ALKALI
Answer: How the baker won the town election —
IN A CAKEWALK

59. **Jumbles:** PECAN CATCH HAIRDO PREFIX
Answer: What the groom did when he married the math
teacher — CARRIED THE "ONE"

60. **Jumbles:** FAITH VAPOR EXODUS HANDED
Answer: The owner didn't repair the roof because it was —
OVER HIS HEAD

61. **Jumbles:** SHAKY AROMA TOUCHY LEGUME
Answer: The kind of dress worn by a ghost — SEE-THROUGH

62. **Jumbles:** WHOSE BOUGH SCROLL DAMASK
Answer: What he used when he was fishing for a good novel
— A BOOKWORM

63. **Jumbles:** GOURD ALBUM SWERVE HOPPER
Answer: When he rolled a perfect game, he was —
"BOWLED" OVER

64. **Jumbles:** FRIAR AIDED MIDWAY FOIBLE
Answer: How he described his parrot — A WORDY BIRDIE

65. **Jumbles:** WALTZ DUCHY GAINED MISERY
Answer: Where you can find the most fish — IN THE MIDDLE

66. **Jumbles:** PRINT KNAVE GRATIS AGHAST
Answer: What the couple went through buying the right
house — THEIR SAVINGS

67. **Jumbles:** MERGE NUTTY EGOISM JETSAM
Answer: How the couple described the Grand Canyon —
JUST "GORGES"

68. **Jumbles:** AFIRE DITTY USEFUL PIRATE
Answer: What the scout experienced when he hiked through
the woods — A FIELD "TRIP"

69. **Jumbles:** OPERA BANJO TRIBAL SUBWAY
Answer: When the players began fighting, the game turned
into — BASE BRAWL

70. **Jumbles:** NOOSE SHEEP DITHER VIRTUE
Answer: What the sarge said to the sleeping recruit —
RISE AND SHINE

71. **Jumbles:** PUTTY SNARL BEACON BASKET
Answer: What the broker gave the nervous investor —
A "STOCK" REPLY

72. **Jumbles:** JUMPY CHUTE PURVEY JANGLE
Answer: No matter what is served, this will make it
attractive — HUNGER

73. **Jumbles:** TEASE CURRY SPORTY ABUSED
Answer: The mattress was guaranteed so the couple
could — "REST" ASSURED

74. **Jumbles:** ENEMY STEED SPLEEN VOYAGE
Answer: Window-shopping with his wife left him —
"GLASSY" EYED

75. **Jumbles:** PILOT GORGE BUMPER DISCUS
Answer: When the tattoo artist put a butterfly on her leg, she
was — "IMPRESSED"

76. **Jumbles:** HASTY AFTER KOSHER TYPING
Answer: What the hairdresser did for the long-haired
brunette — "SET" HER RIGHT

77. **Jumbles:** HUMAN WEDGE DENOTE HEREBY
Answer: The farmer's simple philosophy was —
DOWN TO "EARTH"

78. **Jumbles:** KNOWN LITHE LIQUOR TROUGH
Answer: What the electrician did while he recovered from his
injury — "LIGHT" WORK

79. **Jumbles:** YACHT IDIOT FLABBY PERMIT
Answer: When they met on horseback, she was on the —
"BRIDAL" PATH

80. **Jumbles:** UNITY BASSO CELERY TIMELY
Answer: The mailman received an advanced degree because
he was a — MAN OF "LETTERS"

81. **Jumbles:** RAPID EMPTY INLAID COUPLE
Answer: What she experienced when she danced in her new
shoes — PAIN AT THE "PUMP"

82. **Jumbles:** POUND PLAID HAUNCH WOEFUL
Answer: The police roadblock led to a — HOLDUP HOLDUP

83. **Jumbles:** JULEP CAMEO PURPLE DEBTOR
Answer: What the farmer saw when he visited the junkyard
— A "BUMPER" CROP

84. **Jumbles:** EVOKE FAULT SINFUL GOLFER
Answer: She chased the real estate developer because he
had — "LOTS" TO OFFER

85. **Jumbles:** ANKLE HITCH BAKERY KITTEN
Answer: What she thought when their paths crossed on the
trail — TAKE A HIKE

86. **Jumbles:** LINGO ARDOR MARTIN KENNEL
Answer: Wise to do when it's "love at first sight" —
LOOK AGAIN

87. **Jumbles:** LILAC ACUTE UNCOIL TYCOON
Answer: Where the actor was shot in the movie —
ON LOCATION

88. **Jumbles:** QUEEN RIVET BANANA COMPLY
Answer: Used for taste when eating — A PALATE

89. **Jumbles:** JUDGE PIECE BRANCH POSTAL
Answer: What Mom did when her son needed a Halloween
costume — "SCARED" ONE UP

90. **Jumbles:** AWFUL DOGMA FROZEN COUSIN
Answer: Lots of people make them at a ball game —
CROWDS

91. **Jumbles:** LARVA DERBY BODILY COOPER
Answer: Sitting through a lengthy presentation made the
directors a — BORED BOARD

92. **Jumbles:** YODEL COMET MULISH TALKER
Answer: What the grocer did to the lazy bag boy —
"SACKED" HIM

93. **Jumbles:** NERVY BLIMP OPAQUE FUNGUS
Answer: When she wanted an expensive new bed, her
husband decided to — SLEEP ON IT

94. **Jumbles:** EIGHT AGILE WHITEN UNCLAD
Answer: A good way to begin a poker tournament —
WITH A HAND

95. **Jumbles:** PENCE QUASH UPSHOT FEWEST
Answer: When the doorman was arrested, the detective had
an — OPEN AND SHUT CASE

96. **Jumbles:** JERKY PROXY BENUMB MUSCLE
Answer: When the plumber gave him the bill, he was close
to — "PLUMB" BROKE

97. **Jumbles:** YOKEL GASSY FLIMSY ABLAZE
Answer: Why the wanderer didn't enjoy hunting —
HE WAS "AIMLESS"

98. **Jumbles:** LYING INLET REBUKE BEHIND
Answer: The scouts gathered wood because they had a —
"BURNING" NEED

99. **Jumbles:** BEFIT HOBBY SECOND LIMBER
Answer: Where the brawling hotheads ended up —
IN THE "COOLER"

100. **Jumbles:** REARM TRILL PLOWED BAFFLE
Answer: He left the restaurant when the hostess said he had
a — "WAIT" PROBLEM

101. **Jumbles:** SHOWY MOURN GAIETY DAMPEN
Answer: When the beauty queen was crowned, it was a —
"HEADY" MOMENT

102. **Jumbles:** FOYER BLOOM EXPEND SOOTHE
Answer: "Robes" all mixed up can be — SOBER

103. **Jumbles:** ITCHY ARMOR IMPACT DEFILE
Answer: For a gambler, playing craps can be — "PAIR-A-DICE"

104. **Jumbles:** FILMY ELOPE INLAND HICCUP
Answer: What the acupuncturist did when he treated the
wrestler — "PINNED" HIM

105. **Jumbles:** BROOK TUNED LADING OSSIFY
Answer: A successful dress designer is good with this —
"FIGURES"

106. **Jumbles:** GUMMY NOVEL UPLIFT UNLOAD
Answer: What the climbers achieved when they reached the
summit — A "LOFTY" GOAL

107. **Jumbles:** COWER BUXOM ANYONE BICKER
Answer: What the reporter got from the editor —
MORE WORK

108. **Jumbles:** SMOKY FACET HORROR SNAPPY
Answer: What it takes to learn about the stars —
ASTRONOMY

109. **Jumbles:** CRACK TESTY BARREN PUNDIT
Answer: Training for submarine duty has to be —
UNDERTAKEN

110. **Jumbles:** SUITE DUCAT SLOUCH POTENT
Answer: The butcher was let go because he —
COULDN'T "CUT" IT

111. **Jumbles:** SNOWY COLON BAMBOO AERATE
Answer: When the partners argued over use of their yacht, it
turned into — A "ROW" BOAT

112. **Jumbles:** AGING DOUGH LOTION OMELET
Answer: What the indifferent student said when he got a
zero on the test — "NOTHING" TO IT

113. **Jumbles:** TIGER FENCE PICNIC FELONY
Answer: He changed the oil in his wife's car to avoid this —
"FRICTION"

114. **Jumbles:** CARGO TOXIN PEWTER BOYISH
Answer: The songwriter was in demand because his work
was — "NOTE"WORTHY

115. **Jumbles:** MUSTY RAVEN SOCKET DEVICE
Answer: What the flies passed on the movie set —
THE "SCREEN" TEST

116. **Jumbles:** SUEDE PANDA TAMPER PRISON
Answer: Mattresses can provide this —
MEANS OF "SUPPORT"

117. **Jumbles:** OAKEN NEWSY STODGY GROTTO
Answer: Why their boat floated away — KNOTS NOTS

118. **Jumbles:** TOPAZ BELIE ADAGIO PEOPLE
Answer: A good way to get in the last word — APOLOGIZE

119. **Jumbles:** BATHE BOUND POLICE FROSTY
Answer: What it takes to make Dad a soft touch —
A SOFT TOUCH

120. **Jumbles:** HAIRY DUNCE JOCUND FALLEN
Answer: Where they went to meet handsome cowboys —
TO A "DUDE" RANCH

121. **Jumbles:** CLOUT PARTY AGENCY LANCER
Answer: What the watcher saw when he spotted the sea bird
— A TERN TURN

122. **Jumbles:** FRANC ANISE MUSKET FIDDLE
Answer: What he ended up with when he bumped the
doctor's luxury car — "SIDE" EFFECTS

123. **Jumbles:** DRAWL CHIME WHALER ANGINA
Answer: What the cowboy who repaired the truck turned
into — A "WRENCH" HAND

124. **Jumbles:** BARON HABIT ENTIRE FEEBLE
Answer: When the boxer lost the fight, he didn't get up —
BEFORE TEN

125. **Jumbles:** SOGGY AVAIL PIGEON CANOPY
Answer: When they married in haste, they ended up —
ELOPING

126. **Jumbles:** FROZE SHINY DECODE LEGACY
Answer: What the daredevil experienced when he trimmed
the bushes — LIFE ON THE "HEDGE"

127. **Jumbles:** UPPER FLOUR OPENLY VENDOR
Answer: What the skin doctor did when he examined the
patient — "PORED" OVER HIM

128. **Jumbles:** GNARL BRAIN LUNACY MOROSE
Answer: When his cursor failed, the reporter became a —
CURSER

129. **Jumbles:** BOGUS CHICK EXTANT HOURLY
Answer: What happened when they kept drinking to their
health — THEY GOT SICK

130. **Jumbles:** OCTET BASIN VESTRY EITHER
Answer: What it can mean when a husband brings home
flowers for "no reason" — THERE'S A REASON

131. **Jumbles:** RHYME CAMEO CANYON FORCED
Answer: What she hoped to develop with the trainer —
A ROMANCE

132. **Jumbles:** ENACT LOGIC UNWISE VARIED
Answer: Why the banker didn't have many friends —
HE WAS A "LOANER"

133. **Jumbles:** CHEEK MINUS GIGOLO FROTHY
Answer: What the tired gardener planted — HIMSELF

134. **Jumbles:** EXERT ROBOT TOTTER RUBBER
Answer: When the gambler took poker lessons, he became
a — BETTER BETTOR

135. **Jumbles:** CREEK HOARD FUMBLE ALPACA
Answer: When the chef tried a new dish, the diners said it
was — HALF BAKED

136. **Jumbles:** ABOVE CHAIR AFFIRM UNFOLD
Answer: What the executive and politician had in common
— RAN FOR OFFICE

137. **Jumbles:** AGONY LADLE PALATE BYWORD
Answer: How the lonely bank robber felt when he saw his
poster — WANTED

138. **Jumbles:** GLADE ABYSS TINKLE BAKING
Answer: What the poker group played for — BIG STEAKS

139. **Jumbles:** PLUSH CROUP ROBBER EQUATE
Answer: How long did it take the commuter to get to work?
— ABOUT AN HOUR

140. **Jumbles:** SKULK TWEAK ROSARY BARROW
Answer: What a watch repairer does — WORKS THE WORKS

141. **Jumbles:** AWASH GAVEL OUTWIT DOUBLY
Answer: He turned out to be a bigamist because he loved —
TWO WELL

142. **Jumbles:** AIDED OPIUM NICELY HAZING
Answer: What the street artist drew — AN AUDIENCE

143. **Jumbles:** FLUTE HASTY SWERVE RAMROD
Answer: To some, the banker's son was worth a lot, to others
he was — WORTHLESS

144. **Jumbles:** OLDER BEFOG POROUS FORGOT
Answer: What a comfortable shoe can be —
GOOD FOR THE SOLE

145. **Jumbles:** WHINE POACH IMPORT FAMOUS
Answer: When they raced to develop the news pictures, it
was a — PHOTO "FINISH"

146. **Jumbles:** COLIC BULLY GARISH SEPTIC
Answer: What the retiree needed when he decided to take
up golf — A "COURSE"

147. **Jumbles:** SHEEP TULLE LAVISH POPLIN
    Answer: The shop owner's donut discount amounted to — "HOLE" SALE
148. **Jumbles:** PUTTY GIVEN PEPSIN BANISH
    Answer: What the eye doctor required for his new office building — A SIGHT SITE
149. **Jumbles:** EVENT MADAM TOWARD NOVICE
    Answer: What the mobsters experienced when they went surfing — A CRIME "WAVE"
150. **Jumbles:** QUAKE KNOWN CANNED ACTUAL
    Answer: When the noisy pet duck woke up the farmboy, it was the — "QUACK" OF DAWN
151. **Jumbles:** LIMBO OXIDE KOSHER EGOISM
    Answer: This helped the pretty biologist get ahead — HER GOOD "LOOKS"
152. **Jumbles:** AROMA WEDGE MISERY PEPTIC
    Answer: What the convict sought at the prison library — A WAY TO "ESCAPE"
153. **Jumbles:** SURLY GORGE PILFER BLOODY
    Answer: The young witch joined the bee contestants because she was — A GOOD "SPELLER"
154. **Jumbles:** MERGE TWINE MYSELF JITNEY
    Answer: How the teens got along when they met at the pool — "SWIMMINGLY"
155. **Jumbles:** DUMPY LEGAL CASKET GUZZLE
    Answer: What the rower suffered when his boat hit the pier — SCULL DAMAGE
156. **Jumbles:** GAUGE LYRIC FUTILE THRASH
    Answer: When the beauty queen became a witch for Halloween, she was a — "FRIGHT"
157. **Jumbles:** FLORA CROWN AVENUE EMPLOY
    Answer: The paper hangers worked late because they — WERE ON A "ROLL"
158. **Jumbles:** LATCH EMPTY PUDDLE BEACON
    Answer: What the second base umpire got after the game — HOME "PLATE"
159. **Jumbles:** CLUCK BELLE ALKALI BUZZER
    Answer: The boxer entered the ring wearing red and white and left — BLACK AND BLUE
160. **Jumbles:** ABHOR ORBIT DAMASK MISFIT
    Answer: Trouble in a joint can mean this — ARTHRITIS
161. **Jumbles:** MOBILE SUGARY MUSEUM VANDAL BALLAD HYMNAL
    Answer: This is true no matter how long a calendar is kept — ITS DAYS ARE "NUMBERED"
162. **Jumbles:** TURNIP LATEST GEYSER PLENTY DARING CEMENT
    Answer: When he lost his voice, the doctor gave him the — "SILENT" TREATMENT
163. **Jumbles:** FILLET SURTAX TINKLE GUZZLE PURIFY POETRY
    Answer: When the model posed in the easy chair, she was — SITTING "PRETTY"
164. **Jumbles:** INSIST FEUDAL REDEEM DRUDGE BLOODY BUZZER
    Answer: When the race horses kept losing, their owner was — "SADDLED" WITH DEBT
165. **Jumbles:** NIPPLE OBTUSE CARNAL ROBBER UTMOST PANTRY
    Answer: What the buyer offered when the saleswoman showed him a tie — A "COUNTER" PROPOSAL
166. **Jumbles:** CALMLY HOMING COBALT FESTAL ISLAND HAMLET
    Answer: What it took to get his son through college — ALMOST ALL HE HAD
167. **Jumbles:** NEGATE BALLET CLAUSE UNIQUE HELMET ANSWER
    Answer: When he got holes in his socks, he said they were on — THEIR "LAST LEGS"
168. **Jumbles:** RENDER JACKAL EYELET ANKLET CARPET BEHELD
    Answer: What the musician did when he became a policeman — LEARNED THE "BEAT"
169. **Jumbles:** INFIRM LEEWAY ARMORY BOTANY HERESY EMERGE
    Answer: What some men can end up knitting — THEIR EYEBROWS
170. **Jumbles:** CYMBAL NEARBY FIERCE PREACH MISLAY MENACE
    Answer: These can make your feet hurt when visiting ancient ruins — FALLEN "ARCHES"
171. **Jumbles:** CUPFUL NAUSEA METRIC GIMLET QUAINT EMBARK
    Answer: When the couple reconciled, they said the marriage counselor was a — "MAKEUP" ARTIST
172. **Jumbles:** DOOMED KNOTTY SNUGLY STOLID LAWFUL JINGLE
    Answer: Their extended good-bye turned into a — SO LONG "SO-LONG"
173. **Jumbles:** FUTURE LOUNGE BEAUTY GADFLY INFUSE SUBURB
    Answer: What busy ladies did during the Victorian era — "BUSTLED" ABOUT
174. **Jumbles:** OCELOT VIOLIN RACIAL HINDER BETRAY GIGGLE
    Answer: When the groom was late, the bride made a— "VEILED" THREAT
175. **Jumbles:** HOOKUP VANISH TIMING FINERY POETIC WHENCE
    Answer: What the guard said when he approached the haunted house — "WHO 'GHOST' THERE?"
176. **Jumbles:** ORIOLE STUDIO POLISH WORTHY HEARSE MORGUE
    Answer: Wearing a tie to a fancy casino doesn't mean you won't do this — LOSE YOUR SHIRT
177. **Jumbles:** FIGURE DEPICT FELLOW WEASEL GUIDED NOODLE
    Answer: What the swimmers did to win the relay race — "POOLED" THEIR EFFORTS
178. **Jumbles:** INJURY ADRIFT SATIRE MYRIAD DIVERT VORTEX
    Answer: The historian returned to his alma mater because he was a — "FORMER" STUDENT
179. **Jumbles:** CABANA BARREL NIMBLE GOITER SHAKEN LOCATE
    Answer: Difficult for a big-time bettor to do — BALANCE HIS BOOKIES
180. **Jumbles:** WINNOW SUBMIT TURGID SAVORY RAREFY ECZEMA
    Answer: When the pub crawler heard the drinking song, it was — GOOD FOR A FEW "BARS"

Need More Jumbles®?

Jumble® Books

More than 175 puzzles each!

Jammin' Jumble®
$9.95 • ISBN: 1-57243-844-4

Java Jumble®
$9.95 • ISBN: 978-1-60078-415-6

Jazzy Jumble®
$9.95 • ISBN: 978-1-57243-962-7

Jet Set Jumble®
$9.95 • ISBN: 978-1-60078-353-1

Joyful Jumble®
$9.95 • ISBN: 978-1-60078-079-0

Juke Joint Jumble®
$9.95 • ISBN: 978-1-60078-295-4

Jumble® at Work
$9.95 • ISBN: 1-57243-147-4

Jumble® Celebration
$9.95 • ISBN: 978-1-60078-134-6

Jumble® Explosion
$9.95 • ISBN: 978-1-60078-078-3

Jumble® Fever
$9.95 • ISBN: 1-57243-593-3

Jumble® Fiesta
$9.95 • ISBN: 1-57243-626-3

Jumble® Fun
$9.95 • ISBN: 1-57243-379-5

Jumble® Galaxy
$9.95 • ISBN: 978-1-60078-583-2

Jumble® Genius
$9.95 • ISBN: 1-57243-896-7

Jumble® Getaway
$9.95 • ISBN: 978-1-60078-547-4

Jumble® Grab Bag
$9.95 • ISBN: 1-57243-273-X

Jumble® Jackpot
$9.95 • ISBN: 1-57243-897-5

Jumble® Jambalaya
$9.95 • ISBN: 978-1-60078-294-7

Jumble® Jamboree
$9.95 • ISBN: 1-57243-696-4

Jumble® Jitterbug
$9.95 • ISBN: 978-1-60078-584-9

Jumble® Jubilee
$9.95 • ISBN: 1-57243-231-4

Jumble® Juggernaut
$9.95 • ISBN: 978-1-60078-026-4

Jumble® Junction
$9.95 • ISBN: 1-57243-380-9

Jumble® Jungle
$9.95 • ISBN: 978-1-57243-961-0

Jumble® Madness
$9.95 • ISBN: 1-892049-24-4

Jumble® Mania
$9.95 • ISBN: 1-57243-697-2

Jumble® See & Search
$9.95 • ISBN: 1-57243-549-6

Jumble® See & Search 2
$9.95 • ISBN: 1-57243-734-0

Jumble® Sensation
$9.95 • ISBN: 978-1-60078-548-1

Jumble® Surprise
$9.95 • ISBN: 1-57243-320-5

Jumpin' Jumble®
$9.95 • ISBN: 978-1-60078-027-1

Outer Space Jumble®
$9.95 • ISBN: 978-1-60078-416-3

Rainy Day Jumble®
$9.95 • ISBN: 978-1-60078-352-4

Ready, Set, Jumble®
$9.95 • ISBN: 978-1-60078-133-0

Sports Jumble®
$9.95 • ISBN: 1-57243-113-X

Summer Fun Jumble®
$9.95 • ISBN: 1-57243-114-8

Travel Jumble®
$9.95 • ISBN: 1-57243-198-9

TV Jumble®
$9.95 • ISBN: 1-57243-461-9

Oversize Jumble® Books

More than 500 puzzles each!

Generous Jumble®
$19.95 • ISBN: 1-57243-385-X

Giant Jumble®
$19.95 • ISBN: 1-57243-349-3

Gigantic Jumble®
$19.95 • ISBN: 1-57243-426-0

Jumbo Jumble®
$19.95 • ISBN: 1-57243-314-0

The Very Best of Jumble® BrainBusters
$19.95 • ISBN: 1-57243-845-2

Jumble® Crosswords™

More than 175 puzzles each!

More Jumble® Crosswords™
$9.95 • ISBN: 1-57243-386-8

Jumble® Crosswords™ Jackpot
$9.95 • ISBN: 1-57243-615-8

Jumble® Crosswords™ Jamboree
$9.95 • ISBN: 1-57243-787-1

Jumble® BrainBusters™

More than 175 puzzles each!

Jumble® BrainBusters™
$9.95 • ISBN: 1-892049-28-7

Jumble® BrainBusters™ II
$9.95 • ISBN: 1-57243-424-4

Jumble® BrainBusters™ III
$9.95 • ISBN: 1-57243-463-5

Jumble® BrainBusters™ IV
$9.95 • ISBN: 1-57243-489-9

Jumble® BrainBusters™ 5
$9.95 • ISBN: 1-57243-548-8

Jumble® BrainBusters™ Bonanza
$9.95 • ISBN: 1-57243-616-6

Boggle™ BrainBusters™
$9.95 • ISBN: 1-57243-592-5

Boggle™ BrainBusters™ 2
$9.95 • ISBN: 1-57243-788-X

Jumble® BrainBusters™ Junior
$9.95 • ISBN: 1-892049-29-5

Jumble® BrainBusters™ Junior II
$9.95 • ISBN: 1-57243-425-2

Fun in the Sun with Jumble® BrainBusters™
$9.95 • ISBN: 1-57243-733-2